Angels

and other Mysteries of
The Tree of Life

Translated from the French
Original title :
DE L'HOMME À DIEU
séphiroth et hiérarchies angéliques

Omraam Mikhaël Aïvanhov

Angels

and other Mysteries of
The Tree of Life

Izvor Collection — No. 236

P R O S V E T A

Canadian Cataloguing in Publication Data

Aïvanhov, Omraam Mikhaël, 1900-1986

Angels and other mysteries of the Tree of Life

(Izvor collection ; 236)
Translation of: De l'homme à Dieu.
ISBN 1-895978-07-6

1. Tree of Life. 2. Angels. I.Title.
II. Series: Izvor collection (Laval, Quebec) ; 236.

BL477.A59 1995   299'.93   C95-900568-4

Prosveta S.A. — B.P. 12 — 83601 Fréjus Cedex (France)

Readers will better understand certain aspects of the lectures published in the present volume if they bear in mind that Master Omraam Mikhaël Aïvanhov's teaching was exclusively oral and that the editors have made every effort to respect the flavour and style of each lecture.

The Master's teaching is more than a body of doctrines; it is an organic whole, and his way of presenting it was to approach it from countless different points of view. By repeating certain aspects in a wide variety of contexts he constantly reveals a new dimension of the whole and at the same time throws new light on the individual aspects and their vital links with each other.

TABLE OF CONTENTS

Chapter One

FROM MAN TO GOD

THE NOTION OF HIERARCHY

Human beings are often like rudderless boats adrift on the tide. Fortunately, thanks to their family, their studies, their profession, or simply their social life, they have a few rules and an external frame of reference to guide them, but inwardly many of them are like little boats floating in mid-ocean without compass or chart. You will say that many people have a religion. That is true, and religion would help them tremendously if its official representatives were able to teach them how to understand and control their inner life. It is not my intention to criticize the churches or the clergy; in any case, many others have already done so with greater eloquence than I could muster. All I want is to show you how to achieve the goal of all religions: to establish a link with God.

It is often said that the word religion comes from the Latin *religare*, meaning to tie or link.

Thus religion is what links us to God. But what is our idea of God, and how is this link established? You will say: 'Oh, that's easy; you can link yourself to God through prayer.' If only it were so simple! If only it were enough to say: 'My Lord and my God...' for us to be immediately in contact with God!

If anyone thinks they can make direct contact with the Lord it shows that they have no notion of who or what God is. I am not saying that we cannot get anywhere near him—we can—but we certainly cannot have direct contact with God in person. A very simple example illustrates this. When you write to a friend, your letter has to be transported by various intermediaries: the employee behind the counter who stamps it, and those who carry it away by road, rail, or air. And when it reaches the town where your friend lives it still has to be carried by a postman, who drops it in your friend's letter-box or gives it to the janitor to give to him. And if you are writing to a very high-ranking person, it will probably end up in the hands of a secretary. And that secretary may or may not hand it on, for if your letter is not really important, it will never reach the dignitary to whom you addressed it. It will be read and answered by one of his assistants.

This is how things are organized on earth, and those who disregard this and think that their messages or prayers will reach the Lord directly are simply ignorant. They know that they cannot approach an important person on earth without going through intermediaries, but they think that the Lord can be approached directly. Oh yes, the Lord is a kindly old fellow; anyone can go up to him and tap him on the shoulder or tweak his beard. He is always ready to listen to all your complaints and petitions, and it is he himself who answers them! How can people be so ignorant as to think that their thoughts and prayers will fly directly up to God, and that he will make a special journey to come and take care of them? Do they think that he is all alone in heaven; that he has no servants or workers to do things for him; that he has to do everything himself? They even think that it was he alone who set to work and created the world in six days... Poor God, what a job that must have been! And with no one to help him.

Even the least important manager or director on earth has one or more secretaries and teams of workers, and yet people imagine that the Lord has to do everything himself, and every Tom, Dick, and Harry can approach him directly. There are people who will tell you in all seriousness that they go and discuss things with God, and he answers them. Or sometimes it is the other way round: God comes and discusses things with them and they give him their opinion! Poor ignorant wretches! If what they imagine actually happened they would have been ground to dust and blasted out of existence long ago. There would be not the tiniest trace of them left on earth. God is an energy of indescribable power; no human being has ever touched, or heard, or seen him. You will say that Abraham, Moses, and the prophets of Israel spoke with God. Yes, the Old Testament recounts many dialogues of this sort, but in reality they are no more than images, figures of speech.

As a matter of fact, there is one image that can give us an approximate idea of God, and that is electricity. We use electricity for light and heat. All kinds of tools and appliances function thanks to electricity. How could our homes, factories, and cities get along without it? But at the same time, as we all know, great care has to be taken to avoid short-circuits or other accidents leading to electrocution or fire. Direct contact with an electric current can be fatal, for it is extremely powerful. When we want to make electricity safe in our homes so that we can use it with a minimum of risk, we have to use transformers to step down its power and pass it through a system of wiring that is sometimes very complicated. Well, the same is true of God. God can be compared to unadulterated electricity, which, in order to be brought down to our level, needs to be passed through transformers. And these transformers are the countless luminous beings who inhabit the heavens, and who are known to tradition as the angelic hierarchies. It is through them that we receive divine light, and it is through them that we can be in contact with God.

Yes, it is very important to know that there is a great distance between us and God, a space so vast, so immense, that no human mind can comprehend it. But that space is not empty: it is made up of different regions that are inhabited by spiritual entities. In their own way, all religions mention the existence of these regions and entities, but to my mind it is the notions contained in the Jewish tradition that are the clearest and most exact. Both Christianity and Islam have inherited some elements of the Jewish tradition.

Most human beings behave as though they were the only highly evolved creatures in existence. Below them, they think, are animals, plants, and minerals, and above them, very far away, is the Lord— always supposing that they believe in him! They have no notion of the existence of all those beings that bridge the gulf between the Lord and ourselves. Or if they know that they exist, because they heard them mentioned in their childhood, they rarely think of them or attempt to make contact with them. Catholic and Orthodox Christians pray to the saints, and this is good, but even the greatest saints are only human beings, and the veneration they receive often resembles pagan idolatry: St Anthony of Padua is called upon to find lost property; St Christopher is asked to protect his devotees from accidents, and so on. Almost all the saints in the calendar have their own special function. There are countless representations of the Virgin Mary, for example, each with its own speciality: to heal the sick, to give protection in danger, to ensure a successful child-birth or a rich harvest, to bring an absent husband or an erring wife home, and so on. Christians tend to despise polytheistic religions with their numerous gods; they do not realize that, in their own way, they, too, have a veritable pantheon.

This custom of invoking spiritual entities who are believed to possess certain specific powers has its origins in the remote past, and Christians have done no more than adopt and prolong it. The fact that they have done so shows that, even for them, God is so far away that they feel the need of intermediaries. This is why it is important to be better informed about the angelic hierarchies; to know what they are, how they relate to God and to ourselves, and what powers they have.

In Genesis we find the story of Jacob's ladder which is a symbol of the angelic hierarchy that links man to God.

> *Jacob came to a certain place and stayed there for the night, because the sun had set. Taking one of the stones of the place, he put it under his head and lay down in that place. And he dreamed that there was a ladder set up on the earth, the top of it reaching to heaven; and there the angels of God were ascending and descending on it. And the Lord stood beside him.*

The notion of a ladder or scale is worth exploring, for it expresses not only the idea of an intermediary between the higher and the lower, but also that of hierarchy. When we speak of a social scale or ladder we are expressing the notion that there is a hierarchy, a difference of degree, in the positions human beings occupy in society. We speak also of a scale of values, a scale of colours, and so on. Everything in life points to the need for ladders or scales, if for no other purpose than to get up to the roof. You will say that there are other means of getting on to the roof. True, but whatever means you use it is the equivalent of a ladder.

The Christian tradition—which follows the Judaic tradition in this—teaches that there are nine orders of angels: Angels, Archangels,

Principalities, Virtues, Powers, Dominations, Thrones, Cherubim, and Seraphim. Each angelic order represents one aspect of the powers and virtues of God. Above all, they represent something that is more accessible to us than the notion of God. Our spiritual development requires that we know about these higher entities, for they are the beacons that light up our path.

Of course, there is no reason why you should not continue to speak to God, but you must realize that you will not reach him directly. He has servants who will transmit your prayers and supplications to him. On the other hand, it is as well to know that these servants may not forward every one of your prayers. Many prayers never reach their destination because the entities in charge of sorting them glance at them and say: 'There is no point in delivering this one to the Lord. He has better things to do than to listen to petitions of this kind. Into the waste-paper basket with it!'

Neither is it any use deluding yourself that God will come and visit you in person. It is possible that an archangel may come and bring you a message, an atom of light, and even that would be an immense grace. Who do we think we are that God, the Lord of the universe, should put himself out to visit us? In any case, if he ever did so, we would not survive the infinitely powerful vibrations of his presence. The Psalms tell us that 'mountains melt like wax before the Lord.' As I have said, the angelic hierarchies are the transformers that step down that power so that we can receive it without being pulverized by it.

Yes, let this be quite clear in your minds: there is, of course, no reason why you should not speak directly to God—I do so myself—as long as you know that your prayers will be carried to him by other beings, and that if they are not truly pure and unselfish they will be thrown into the waste-paper basket. They will not be answered. It is better to know in advance how these things work. In this way you need not delude yourselves or wait in vain for an answer. We can receive no more than a ray of light, a faint fragrance from far, far away that filters down through the angelic hierarchies to us. It is always God who answers us, for God is present on every level of his creation, but he does not answer us directly.

Chapter Two

INTRODUCTION TO THE

SEPHIROTIC TREE OF LIFE

For those who feel the need to approach the Creator, to try to penetrate his immensity, religion provides a variety of means among which are prayer, the attendance at religious ceremonies, and obedience to certain rules. These means are good but they are insufficient. If you want to come closer to God, it is not enough to experience mystical emotions and abide by certain rules: you also need the profound understanding of the universe which only a systematic explanation can give you.

Very early on in life I wanted to find such a system and searched for it everywhere, in the teachings of all the great religions of mankind. It was in the Jewish tradition of the Cabbalah, in what is known as the Sephirotic Tree, or Tree of life, that I found what seemed to me to be the best and most complete system, for it is the farthest-reaching and the most exact. I am not saying that other doctrines are bad or false, but the notions they present are fragmented. They do not give such a profound, well-structured, synthetic view of the whole. The Sephirotic Tree is a veritable synthesis of the universe. For me, it is the key that enables us to unlock the mysteries of creation. The visual symbol is extremely simple, but the contents are inexhaustible. Many episodes recounted in the Old and New Testaments can be understood only in the light of the Sephirotic Tree.

Cabbalists divide the universe into ten regions or sephiroth, which correspond to the numbers one to ten (the word *sephirah*, plural *sephiroth*, means numeration). Each sephirah is identified by five names: the name of God, the name of the sephirah itself, the name of the leader of the angelic order, the name of the angelic order, and, finally, the name of one of the planets.[1]

Thus each sephirah includes five distinct planes of being, and you will better understand the nature of these five different planes if you know that they correspond to the five principles in man: the spirit, soul, intellect, heart, and physical body. The divine plane corresponds to the human spirit; that of the sephirah to the soul; the leader of the angelic order corresponds to the intellect; the angelic order to

---

[1] A colour plate of the Sephirotic Tree at the end of this volume can be consulted to help clarify these explanations.

the heart, and the planet to the physical body.

Thus each sephirah is a region inhabited by an order of luminous spirits under the leadership of an archangel, who is directly subject to God. Of course, it is God who governs the ten regions, but under a different name in each. This is why the Cabbalah says that God has ten names. These ten names correspond to ten different attributes. God is one, but he manifests himself differently according to the region. It is always one and the same God, seen under ten different aspects, and each aspect is equal—neither inferior nor superior—to all the others.

The ten names of God are:

Ehieh	*Eloha va Daath*
Yah	*Jehovah Tzebaoth*
Jehovah	*Elohim Tzebaoth*
El	*Shaddai El Hai*
Elohim Gibor	*Adonai Melek* [2]

The names of the ten sephiroth are:

Kether	Crown	*Tiphareth*	Beauty
Chokmah	Wisdom	*Netzach*	Victory
Binah	Understanding	*Hod*	Glory
Chesed	Mercy	*Yesod*	Foundation
Geburah	Strength	*Malkuth*	Kingdom

---

[2] For the meaning of these names see chapter 6.

The leaders of the angelic orders are:

Metatron	He who stands by the throne
Raziel	Secret of God
Tzaphkiel	Contemplation of God
Tzadkiel	Justice of God
Kamaël	Desire of God
Mikhaël	Who is Like God?
Haniel	Grace of God
Raphaël	Healing of God
Gabriel	Power of God
Uriel	God is my Light; or

Sandalfon, who is seen as the force that binds matter to form.

The angelic orders are:

Hayoth HaKadesh	Holy Living Creatures, or Seraphim
Ophanim	Wheels, or Cherubim
Aralim	Lions, or Thrones
Hashmalim	Shining Ones, or Dominations
Seraphim	Fiery Ones, or Powers
Malakhim	Kings, or Virtues
Elohim	Gods, or Principalities
Bnei Elohim	Sons of the Gods, or Archangels
Kerubim	Strong Ones, or Angels
Ishim	Men, or the Communion of Saints

Finally the cosmic bodies or planets, which correspond to our physical body:

Rashith HaGalgalim	First Swirlings
Mazloth	The Zodiac
Shabbathai	Saturn
Tzedek	Jupiter
Maadim	Mars
Shemesh	Sun
Noga	Venus
Kokab	Mercury
Levanah	Moon
Aretz	Earth; or
Olem HaYesodoth	World of Foundations

The Ancients, who knew only seven planets, did not include Uranus, Neptune, or Pluto on the Sephirotic Tree. They attributed the nebulae, or first swirlings (*Rashith Ha-Galgalim*), to Kether, and the Zodiac (*Mazloth*) to Chokmah. We can retain these attributions, but we can also place Uranus in Chokmah, Pluto in Daath,[3] and Neptune in Kether.

Why did the cabbalists call this figure the Tree of Life? Because the ten sephiroth have to be seen as an organic whole and can best be understood by comparison with a tree.

---

[3] See pages 33 and 113 for an explanation of the sephirah Daath.

How is a tree constituted? It has roots, a trunk, branches, leaves, flowers, and fruit, and all these elements are interdependent. Similarly, the sephiroth are linked to each other by channels of communication known as 'paths'. These paths, twenty-two in all, are designated by the twenty-two letters of the Hebrew alphabet:

א	Aleph	ל	Lamed
ב	Bet	מ	Mem
ג	Gimmel	נ	Nun
ד	Dalet	ס	Samekh
ה	Heh	ע	Ayin
ו	Vau	פ	Peh
ז	Zayin	צ	Tzadi
ח	Chet	ק	Qof
ט	Tet	ר	Resh
י	Yod	ש	Shin
כ	Kaph	ת	Tav [4]

The twenty-two paths and ten sephiroth add up to what is known as the thirty-two 'paths of wisdom', which belong symbolically in Chokmah. You will better understand the nature and function of these thirty-two paths if you see that they relate to the thirty-two teeth of a human being. Indeed, do we not speak of

[4] The names of the five aspects of each sephirah are given in Hebrew characters alongside the illustration of the Sephirotic Tree at the end of this volume.

wisdom teeth? We have thirty-two teeth with which to chew our food, and the thirty-two paths can be seen metaphorically as teeth with which we chew the psychic and spiritual nourishment we receive each day. It is by means of such spiritual 'mastication' that we acquire wisdom. To become wise is to chew the experiences we encounter each day so as to extract the nutrients they contain.

The thirty-two paths of wisdom link the ten sephiroth, each of which has five divisions. Thus the Cabbalah speaks of the fifty gates of intelligence or understanding, and these gates are attributed symbolically to the sephirah Binah. But in order to open a gate we need a key, and according to initiatic science the true key is self-knowledge. Initiates can know everything because they know themselves. In certain ancient paintings—the frescos in the Egyptian tombs, for instance—one often sees an initiate depicted with a kind of key which resembles the symbol for Venus ♀. As you can see, this symbol represents the simplified figure of a human being, with the head, the outstretched arms, and the two legs joined. The initiates possess the key that enables them to know themselves, and knowing themselves they can know the whole universe; they can open the gates of all regions.

Now you will perhaps be wondering: 'Why ten sephiroth? Is the universe really divided into ten regions?' No, it is not, and this raises a very important point that you must understand. The Sephirotic Tree is designed to teach neither astronomy nor cosmology. The truth is that no one can say exactly what the universe is or how it was created. The Sephirotic Tree represents a systematic world-view that is mystical in nature, and whose origins can be traced back thousands of years. The exceptional beings who conceived it had no telescopes or long-distance lenses through which to study the stars. It was through meditation, contemplation, and the intensity of their inner life that they were able to grasp the cosmic reality and render it intelligible · with the help of images and symbolic descriptions. And it is the essential elements of this tradition, constantly recaptured and meditated upon throughout the ages, that have been handed down to us. So, as I say, the Sephirotic Tree is not an exact description of our universe; and this explains the absence of certain planets, the position of the Sun, and so on.

But to get back to the ten sephiroth: why ten? Because the number ten represents completeness, an accomplished whole. The word sephirah, as I have already explained, means numeration. All numerical combinations stem from the first ten numbers. In the beginning God created ten numbers, the ten sephiroth, and with these ten numbers he can create other numbers, that is, an infinite variety of other beings.

Cabbalists also acknowledge the existence of an eleventh sephirah, *Daath*, whose name means 'knowledge'. *Daath* is situated between *Kether* and *Tiphareth*, but it is rarely mentioned or shown in representations of the Sephirotic Tree.

Now, if you look at a representation of the Sephirotic Tree, you will see that it includes only the powers of good. Those who wish to work towards perfection should study and concentrate only on these. But it is true that the Cabbalah also mentions the *kliphoth*, the ten sephiroth of darkness, which are the inverted reflection of the divine sephiroth, just as Satan is the inverted reflection of God. Each of these malevolent sephiroth has its name and its hierarchy of spiritual denizens, but I shall not go into details about them or even mention their names, for I have no wish to link myself to them in any way.

Finally, cabbalists speak of yet another region beyond *Kether*, the region of *Ain Soph Aur*, limitless light, the region of the Absolute, of the unmanifest God.

The teaching of the Cabbalah sees the universe as an integrated whole, of which the Sephirotic Tree is the perfect expression. Within that whole, however, several different regions can be distinguished.

A first division distinguishes four planes.

The higher plane is *Olam Atziluth*, the world of emanations, and it comprises *Kether, Chokmah* and *Binah*.

Below this is *Olam Briah*, the world of creation, comprising *Chesed*, *Geburah,* and *Tiphareth*.

Below this again is *Olam Yetzirah,* the world of formation, comprising *Netzach*, *Hod,* and *Yesod*.

Finally, there is *Olam Assiah*, the world of action, formed by *Malkuth* alone.

As we see, there is a hierarchy between the world above and the world below, and this hierarchy is reflected in the composition of human beings:

Neshamah, the divine plane of soul and spirit, corresponds to *Olam Atziluth*.

Ruah, the intellect or mental plane, corresponds to *Olam Briah*.

Nephesh, the heart or astral plane, corresponds to *Olam Yetzirah*.

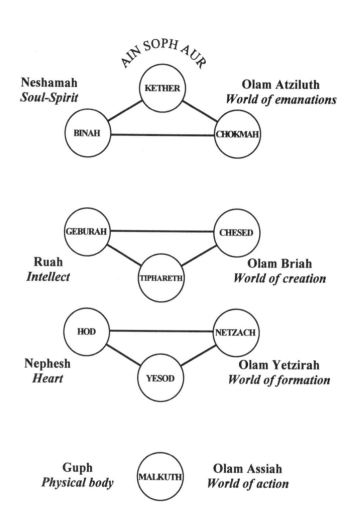

Figure 1

Guph, the physical body, corresponds to *Olam Assiah*.[5]

Another way of dividing the Sephirotic Tree is based on the three pillars.

On the right, *Yakin*, the Pillar of Mercy, is a positive, active power, comprising the three sephiroth *Chokmah*, *Chesed*, and *Netzach*.

On the left, *Boaz*, the Pillar of Severity, is a feminine, passive power, comprising *Binah*, *Geburah*, and *Hod*.

Lastly, the central Pillar, which ensures the balance between left and right, comprises *Kether*, *Daath*, *Tiphareth*, *Yesod*, and *Malkuth*.

This division expresses the notion that the universe is governed by the two opposing principles of masculine and feminine, attraction and repulsion, love and hate, mercy and severity, and that in order to be reconciled and work together in harmony, they have to meet in the centre.[6]

There, you are now in possession of all the essential elements of the Sephirotic Tree. What will you do with them? When an instructor introduces human beings into the sanctuary of the Deity in this way he is taking on a very grave responsibility, for he knows that not many are capable of understanding and using

---

[5] See Figure 1.
[6] See Figure 2.

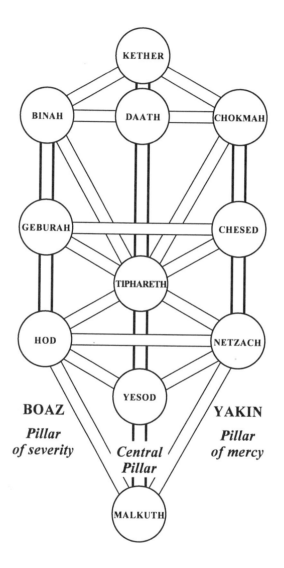

Figure 2

these notions in the right way. Quite apart from
those who will try to use them in the worst
kinds of magical practices, there are many who,
failing to understand their sacred nature, will
imagine that they can stroll among these names
as they would stroll through a public park, and
juggle with the sephiroth as though they were
balls. You must approach this knowledge with
great humility and reverence if you are to gain
any real enlightenment from it.

It is not enough just to read these figures
two or three times and to memorize the names
so that you can use them every now and then in
your conversations. If it is to become the
foundation of some genuine spiritual work, the
Sephirotic Tree must be a permanent subject of
meditation. Try gradually to assimilate and
digest these notions. And you need not be
astonished to hear me using terms that apply to
the field of nutrition. This constant meditation
on the Sephirotic Tree can very aptly be
compared with the process of nutrition. You eat
every day in order to remain healthy, and from
a great variety of foods you choose a few,
which vary from day to day. In the Sephirotic
Tree, too, you will find an extraordinary variety
of 'foods', for it is a reflection of the whole
universe. In it you will, of course, find religion
and philosophy as well as genuine ethics; but it
also contains the sciences and the arts. It is up

to you to learn to find your nourishment in it every day.

It is perfectly true that many saints and mystics have made great spiritual progress without knowing the Sephirotic Tree, but to know it gives one a clearer view of the work that needs to be done. It is a method that can accompany you through life. No other picture or representation surpasses the Sephirotic Tree. Use it faithfully, and your thoughts will no longer stray haphazardly; the blessings it brings you will gradually become more and more abundant as you practise and advance along this path. By reverting frequently to the Sephirotic Tree you will be lighting your inner lamps, and those lamps will not only illuminate you, but will also purify and strengthen you; they will also make you more beautiful and alive. It may well be that you will never fully understand this symbol. It is even more likely that you will never succeed in realizing all the virtues and powers it represents, but it will always be there as the representation of an ideal world that is leading you continually to greater heights.

Chapter Three

THE ANGELIC HIERARCHIES

I

The angels of the sephirah *Kether* are the Seraphim, in Hebrew *Hayoth HaKadesh*, which is translated as Holy Living Creatures. *Hayoth* is the plural of *haya* which means life.

At the beginning of the Book of Ezekiel in the Old Testament there is a description of the four Holy Living Creatures, which is very similar to the one given by St John in the Book of Revelations:

> At once I was in the spirit, and there in heaven stood a throne, with one seated on the throne... Around the throne, and on each side of the throne, are four living creatures full of eyes in front and behind: the first living creature like a lion, the second living creature like an ox, the third living creature with a face like a human face, and the fourth living creature like a

*flying eagle. And the four living creatures,
each of them with six wings, are full of
eyes all around and inside. Day or night
without ceasing they sing,*
'Holy, holy, holy, the Lord God the
Almighty, who was and is and is to come!'

The four Holy Living Creatures before the
throne of God represent the four principles of
matter, the four elements. The lion represents
fire; the ox, earth; the man, air, and the eagle,
water. Matter has its roots, therefore, in God, in
the sephirah *Kether*, and the Seraphim are the
angels of the four elements. But on this plane,
the purity of matter is such that it is almost the
same substance as the spirit.

The Seraphim are the first to receive the
divine emanations. Immersed as they are in the
ocean of primal matter still in a state of
turmoil, they drink at the source of light, the
source of love. This is their only nourishment,
the contemplation of the Lord, and this is why
they are represented as having eyes over the
whole of their bodies. The Seraphim are the
most perfect manifestation of love, for true love
is contemplation.

Actually, there are other expressions of love
in the Sephirotic Tree. *Chesed* (Jupiter), for
instance, represents the love of the community,
and *Netzach* (Venus), love of a creature. But

the love of God, the only true love, can be manifested only in *Kether*, and this is the love of the Seraphim.

Standing before the throne of God, the Seraphim repeat unceasingly: 'Holy, holy, holy, the Lord God the Almighty.' This means that 'holy' is the one word that best expresses the essence of the Deity. Unfortunately, it has been used so often in speaking of men and women who have manifested a certain degree of patience, kindness, or compassion that it has lost its true meaning. If we want to understand what holiness is we have to refer to the Slavic languages. In Bulgarian, for instance, the words holy (*svet*) and holiness (*svetost*) have the same root as the word for light (*svetlina*). Thus holiness is a quality of light. In this sense one can say that only God is truly holy, because he is pure light. This is what the Seraphim are saying, and this is why the word holiness is an integral part of their name: *Hayoth HaKadesh*, creatures of holiness or Holy Living Creatures.

The head of the angelic order of the Seraphim is *Metatron*, the Prince of the Face. As his name indicates, *Metatron* is the only creature who can see God face to face, and it was he who spoke to Moses on Mount Sinai. No human being, however exalted, can be in direct contact with God, for God is a consuming fire that would immediately reduce them to ashes. Human beings always need an intermediary who can speak to them on behalf of God. Even though the Bible says that God spoke to Abraham, Moses, Jacob, or one of the other prophets, in reality it was not God who spoke to them, but a messenger. And this is precisely the meaning of the word 'angel': messenger or emissary.

The angels of *Chokmah* are the Cherubim, known in Hebrew as the *Ophanim*, which means Wheels. The prophet Ezekiel describes his vision of the 'tall and awesome' Wheels that accompanied the living creatures:

> *When the living creatures moved, the wheels moved beside them; and when the living creatures rose from the earth, the wheels rose. Wherever the spirit would go, they went, and the wheels rose along with them; for the spirit of the living creatures was in the wheels. When they moved, the others moved; and when they stopped, the others stopped; and when they rose from the earth, the wheels rose along with them; for the spirit of the living creatures was in the wheels.*

The Holy Living Creatures obey the commands of the spirit and communicate movement to the Wheels.

The symbolism of a wheel (a perfect circle in motion) reveals the special function of the

Cherubim, which is to stir up and organize primeval matter—symbolized by the holy creatures—so that it becomes fit to serve God's purpose. This is why the world of the *Ophanim* is said to be the region of the music of the spheres (here, too, we find the idea of a circle or wheel). In this context, of course, music must be understood as meaning more than an arrangement of sounds created by human beings and perceptible to human ears. The term 'music of the spheres' expresses primarily the harmony that unites all the elements of the universe in a concordance founded on the correlation of numbers. Harmony is above all a structure, and it is when this structure descends to the material plane that it becomes a creator of forms. In this sense harmony is the expression of reason, of wisdom; this is why harmony is also identified with the Logos, the divine Word. There can be no harmony, no music, without reason and wisdom. The divine Word, music, and wisdom are one and the same thing.

Unfortunately, I have to admit that very few of those who create or interpret music are capable of living musically. Music, true music, is not that which is produced by instruments or voices, but that which is expressed in harmonious thoughts, feelings, and gestures in all the circumstances of life. This is the music of *Chokmah*.

At the head of the order of the *Ophanim* is the archangel *Raziel*. According to tradition it was *Raziel* who gave Adam a book, the *Sepher Yetzirah*, which revealed the secrets of creation to him. When Adam committed the first fault, however, this book was taken from him.

The angels of *Binah* are the Thrones. Their name in Hebrew, *Aralim,* means Lions. In Revelations St John associates the presence of the Thrones with that of the Holy Living Creatures, the Seraphim:

> *Around the throne are twenty-four thrones, and seated on the thrones are twenty-four elders dressed in white robes, with golden crowns on their heads... Around the throne, and on each side of the throne, are four living creatures full of eyes in front and behind.*

In another passage the Twenty-four Elders address the Lord thus:

> *We give you thanks, Lord God Almighty, who are and who were and who are to come, for you have taken your great power and begun to reign. The nations raged, but your wrath has come, and the time for judging the dead, for rewarding your servants the prophets and saints*

*and all who fear your name, both small
and great, and for destroying those who
destroy the earth.*

In attributing the name Thrones to the
angels of Binah, the Christian religion
emphasizes the notion of stability, whereas the
Hebrew name *Aralim,* Lions, introduces the
notion of judgement. Symbolically, the lion is
related to justice; the Lion of Juda represents
the supreme judge. The Twenty-four Elders are
the lords of destiny: no single thought,
sentiment, or action of man or woman is hidden
from them. It is they who dispense all
punishments and rewards; they who decree the
conditions in which each individual must
reincarnate.

While the Seraphim sing the holiness of
God, the Twenty-four Elders fall down before
him and worship him, saying: 'You are worthy,
our Lord and God, to receive glory and honour
and power, for you created all things, and by
your will they existed and were created.' Just as
the function of the Seraphim is to celebrate the
holiness of God, that of the Twenty-four Elders
is to proclaim the perfection of his will. They,
too, render justice to God by asserting that he
alone is worthy.

At the head of the *Aralim* is the archangel
Tzaphkiel.

Thus the Seraphim, the Cherubim, and the Thrones are the three angelic orders that belong to the supreme triad composed of *Kether*, *Chokmah*, and *Binah*, and it is because of their exalted position that it is they who are most often mentioned in holy scripture.

The angelic orders of the second triad— *Chesed*, *Geburah*, and *Tiphareth*—are:

the Dominations, *Hashmalim* (Shining Ones);

the Powers, *Seraphim* (Fiery Ones);

the Virtues, *Malakhim* (Kings).

These three orders have in common the fact that they express power, and we identify their action with the qualities of the sephiroth in which they dwell.

The Dominations, the angels of *Chesed* (mercy), pour out their blessings under the direction of the archangel *Tzadkiel,* whose name means 'God is my justice.'

The Powers, the angels of *Geburah* (strength), aflame with zeal for the Creator, are under the leadership of *Kamaël*, Desire of God. Their work, which is to restore order wherever it is in danger in the universe, can be compared with that of the human organism as it strives to rid itself of wastes and toxins.

The Virtues, the angels of *Tiphareth* (beauty), are led by the archangel *Mikhaël*. These are the *Malakhim*, the angels that are mentioned in Revelations: 'And there was war in heaven; *Mikhaël* and his angels fought against the dragon.'

The angelic hierarchies of the third triad, composed of *Netzach*, *Hod*, and *Yesod*, are:
the Principalities, *Elohim* (Gods);
the Archangels, *Bnei Elohim* (Sons of the Gods);
the Angels, *Kerubim* (Strong Ones).
The *Elohim*, under the leadership of *Haniel* (Grace of God), represent the entities that created the world, as related in Genesis: '*Bereshith* (in the beginning) *bara* (created) *Elohim* (the gods) *eth-ha-shamaim* (heaven) *ve-eth ha-aretz* (and the earth).' The blueprint for creation was drawn up by the Architect of the universe in *Chokmah*, and the *Elohim* are the workers who constructed the building. An architect's work is to draw up the plans of a building; the realization of the building itself is entrusted to the building contractors and masons. The *Elohim* are the contractors who built the universe.

The *Bnei Elohim* are the bearers of fire. They are under the leadership of the archangel *Raphaël*, whose name means Healing of God.

The *Kerubim* are the bearers of pure life. It is they who are in touch with human beings more often than the other angelic orders simply because they are closer to them. At their head is the archangel *Gabriel*, 'God is my strength'.

Finally we come to the *Ishim*, which the Cabbalah places in the tenth sephirah, *Malkuth*, even though they are not, properly speaking, one of the angelic orders. The *Ishim* are the saints, prophets, initiates, and great masters of all religions; all those who, by their words and the example of their lives, have led human beings along the path of light. They represent the brotherhood of exalted souls known to Christians as the communion of saints. These are beings who came to earth in order to instruct and help human beings, and it is to them that we should turn first of all, for it is thanks to them, to their teaching and their desire to help us and contribute to our evolution, that we have the ability to rise higher on the scale of created beings. According to the Cabbalah, the leader of the *Ishim* is *Sandalfon*, or *Uriel*.

The Seraphim, Cherubim, and Thrones are in direct contact with God. It is through them that the Dominations, Powers, and Virtues receive the divine emanations, which they in turn transmit to human beings, and, below them, to animals, vegetation, and minerals.

The Seraphim are the spirits of divine love.

The Cherubim are the spirits of divine wisdom.

The Thrones are the spirits of divine power.

The Dominations, Powers, and Virtues are a first reflection of that divine love, wisdom, and power. Below them, the Principalities, Archangels, and Angels are a second reflection. And it is up to us now to make the effort to become the third reflection of that divine perfection by learning to work with all the love of our hearts, all the light of our minds, and all the strength of our wills.

II

When you wake up in the morning, why not start your day by thinking of all those creatures of light going up and down between the earth and the throne of God? If you did this, your whole day would be illuminated. Think of them, link yourself to them, contemplate them in your heart and soul, and say their names. When you are in a crowd and you call somebody's name, they hear you and turn to look at you. This is exactly what happens with the entities of the invisible world: if you call their name, they turn and look at you, and in this way you can make contact with them.

By becoming more and more aware of the reality of these higher entities, you become gradually imbued with their virtues, constantly more alive and luminous; your inner world is progressively enriched. At the same time, however, you must continue to be very unassuming, knowing well that many of these entities will be far beyond your reach for a long time yet. Begin by trying to make contact with the saints and initiates, with the great spiritual masters who have been entrusted with the care of humanity. Later you can rise to a higher plane and try to get in touch with the angels, for the angels are nearer to human beings than any of the other angelic orders, and are always ready to listen to them and help them and to answer their prayers. You can also try to invoke the archangels. But to try and make yourself heard by the Principalities and the higher ranks of the angelic hierarchies is useless. There are innumerable worlds in infinite space, all of them inhabited by billions of creatures, and the higher echelons, who have many different tasks in remote areas of the universe, are not in touch with human beings. Those who are more particularly entrusted with the care of human beings are, as I say, the saints, initiates, and great masters: those who have once lived on earth and who, having left it, remember and continue to be attached to human beings; those who still have promises to keep. Disciples need to know of the existence of the higher angelic orders, and they are free to invoke them, but they must understand that if they want their prayers and meditations to show results, they must address entities that are not so far away.

I am obliged to explain this to you so that you do not delude yourselves and think that you can immediately have access to the Thrones, the Cherubim, or the Seraphim. No, the path to these higher echelons is very, very long. You are not ready for it yet. On the other hand, you must keep it always in view, for only the angelic hierarchies can give you elements of the higher worlds with which to nourish your soul and spirit. This is the only way to fulfil the precept Jesus gave us: 'Be perfect, therefore, as your heavenly Father is perfect.' How can we become perfect if we do not unite ourselves to all those beings who embody the divine virtues?

Perfection requires a knowledge of these hierarchies, and the will to work with them. The Angels will give you pure life. The Archangels will give you the sacred fire. The Principalities will enable you to build and organize your inner world. The Powers will give you the courage and audacity you need to defend your ideal. The Dominations will give you generosity and mercy. The Thrones will give you stability and the understanding of the mysteries. The Cherubim will give you wisdom and harmony. The Seraphim will give you love, the love that surpasses all knowledge, the love that is fulfilment and total freedom.

But how can I dare to speak about these entities, before whom it behoves us only to bow in reverent silence? I do so in order to inspire you with the desire to reject the ease of a prosaic, unconscious existence. A person who does not know that these sublime regions exist can be content with a mediocre life. But those who know of their existence sense that all the worthless things most people value so highly are as nothing compared to what exists in this sublime world. Yes, even the most splendid achievements of science, art, and philosophy pale in comparison. We need, at the very least, to know of the existence of these regions inhabited by perfect beings before we can begin to understand how important it is to draw closer to them.

If you do not begin this work while you are here on earth, you will not be able to go on with it in the next world. You have to begin by blazing the trail in this world if you want to advance in the next. The fact that human beings are incarnated on earth gives them a certain superiority over all angels, even the most exalted, and their task is to draw down the virtues of the angelic hierarchies into their physical body so that, one day, it may become the temple of the Deity. Only then will they achieve fulfilment. Human beings are still at the first stages of their development; this is why the angels take care of them with such patience so as to help them to grow up. They know that they are destined for a glorious future. It has even been said that the angels envy human beings! So take heart, for one day the whole of creation will sing a hymn of praise to mankind.

Chapter Four

THE NAMES OF GOD

Ehieh

When God gave Moses the mission of freeing the Hebrews from the yoke of the Egyptians, Moses replied: 'If I come to the Israelites and say to them, "The God of your ancestors has sent me to you," and they ask me, "What is his name?" what shall I say to them?' Then God replied: '*Ehieh Asher Ehieh*' (the literal meaning of which is 'I shall be who I shall be'). And God added: 'Thus you shall say to the Israelites: "I shall be" has sent me to you.'

Thus *Ehieh*, the name of God that corresponds to the sephirah *Kether*, means 'I shall be.' God names himself 'I shall be' in order to show that he has not manifested himself completely. He is the being of sublime becoming, he whom we can neither see, nor hear, nor touch.

Jehovah, Jehovah Tzebaoth, Yah

In both *Binah* and *Netzach* the name of God is *Jehovah*. Actually, this name was invented by Christians who wished to pronounce the *Tetragrammaton*, Yod Heh Vau Heh, יהוה.[1] The *Tetragrammaton* is the most sacred name of God, which Jews may write but never pronounce. When it occurs in a biblical text that they are reading aloud, they substitute the word *Adonai*, meaning the Lord. According to tradition, only the high priest was authorized to pronounce this name, once a year, in the Holy of holies in the Temple. Thus it is the Tetragrammaton that rules in both *Binah* (*Jehovah*) and in *Netzach* (*Jehovah Tzebaoth*).

The word *Tzebaoth* means armies. Thus *Jehovah Tzebaoth* means God of Armies, but the armies in question are not terrestrial: they are the angelic hierarchies.

In *Chokmah*, God is called *Yah*, which is written: *Yod Heh*, יה,[2] and which is thus an abbreviation of the *Tetragrammaton*.

El, Eloha va Daath, Elohim Gibor

In the sephirah *Chesed*, the divine name is *El*, which simply means God and is found in the names *Eloha* and *Elohim*, the plural of

---

[1] See Chapter 4, The Tetragrammaton and the Seventy-two Planetary Spirits, in Complete Works, vol. 32.
[2] Hebrew is written from right to left.

Eloha. The name of God in *Geburah*, *Elohim Gibor*, means Mighty God. In *Tiphareth*, the name of God is *Eloha va Daath*, which means God and Knowledge. In the sephirah *Hod*, God's name is *Elohim Tzebaoth*, meaning God of Armies. These are the celestial armies composed of the choirs of angels and the stars that proclaim his glory.

Shadai El Hai

In the sephirah *Yesod*, the name of God is *Shadai El Hai*, which is translated to mean Almighty (*Shadai*) Living (*Hai*) God (*El*). Actually, the exact meaning of *El Shadai* is God of Mountains. From the beginning of time the notion of a mountain or summit has been associated with the Deity. It is because God is at the summit that he is almighty.

Adonai Melek

In the sephirah *Malkuth*, God is called *Adonai Melek*. *Adonai*, as we have seen, means Lord, and *Melek* means King. We find the word *Melek* in the name *Melchizedek*, which means King of Justice, and in the name of this sephirah, *Malkuth*, which means Kingdom.

Once again, I wish to emphasize the fact that all these different names represent different aspects of the one God, and that no one aspect is either superior or inferior to the others. The vertical organization of the Sephirotic Tree means that there is a base and a summit, but *Elohim Gibor*, for example, is exactly the same God as *Shadai El Hai*, *El*, or *Ehieh*.

Chapter Five

THE SEPHIROTH OF

THE CENTRAL PILLAR

The goal of a spiritual quest is often symbolized by certain objects that are said to be acquired by an initiate in the course of prolonged labours and lengthy travail. A magic wand, the elixir of everlasting life, the universal panacea, the magic mirror, and the philosophers' stone, all of which are found in certain folk traditions, are symbols of the faculties and powers developed or acquired by an initiate. Are they material possessions? Sometimes they are, but that is not what matters. What matters is that an initiate must seek to possess and work with them as qualities and virtues.

These five symbols have certain correspondences with the sephiroth of the central pillar of the Sephirotic Tree. The magic wand corresponds to *Kether*; the magic mirror to *Daath*; the universal panacea to *Tiphareth*; the elixir of everlasting life to *Yesod*, and the

Magic wand

KETHER

DAATH

Magic mirror

TIPHARETH

Universal panacea

YESOD

Elixir of everlasting life

MALKUTH

Philosophers' stone

philosophers' stone to *Malkuth*. You will ask: 'How can we possess these riches? What work is required of us?'

When you try to transform your petty, ordinary, mediocre thoughts and feelings into noble, generous, and unselfish ones you are working with the philosophers' stone (*Malkuth*), which transmutes base metals into gold.

When you regenerate the cells of your body by the purity of your life, you are working with the elixir of everlasting life (*Yesod*).

When you try to communicate light and love to other human beings, you are working with the universal panacea (*Tiphareth*). When you do this, all those around you begin to feel better: their aches and pains leave them, their cares evaporate, and their courage is renewed. This is the effect that certain very good doctors have: their mere presence eases the sufferings of the sick.

When you habitually focus your thoughts on very exalted realities, you receive messages from space, as though the objects and beings you think about were reflected in a mirror (*Daath*).

When you are truly capable of self-mastery, you begin to gain possession of the magic wand that makes you all-powerful (*Kether*). Never forget that you cannot have control over what is outside yourself until you have gained control of your inner being.

There are other symbols in addition to these, and they correspond to the six other sephiroth. The symbol that corresponds to *Hod* (Mercury) is a book. That for *Netzach* (Venus) is a rose. Because of its scent this is the most precious of all flowers, for spiritual entities are always attracted to a subtle perfume. The symbol corresponding to *Geburah* (Mars) is a sword. In order to defend others and oneself from the onslaughts of evil, a sword, symbolically speaking, is indispensable. The symbol associated with *Chesed* (Jupiter) is a crown or tiara, symbol of royalty and of priesthood. To *Binah* (Saturn) is attributed the skeleton with a sickle, symbol of time and eternity.[1] The symbol for *Chokmah* (Uranus) is a wheel or an eye, the all-seeing eye.

It is up to you now to penetrate the deeper meaning of these symbols, and to work to bring them to life within yourselves. If you tried to possess them outwardly, it would probably be in vain; not only would you be wasting your time, but you would be endangering your psychic balance. A symbol must be used only in its proper context, that is, for your own spiritual life, otherwise it can lead to situations

---

[1] See chapter 15 of this volume.

that are clearly ridiculous. For instance, people talk of the philosophers' stone, which transmutes metals into gold, but they remain poor. They talk of the elixir of everlasting life and the universal panacea, but they are always ill. They talk of magic mirrors and magic wands (they even possess them, for they can easily be bought), but they are still blind and powerless. So what do all these things amount to? It is within yourself that you must find the philosophers' stone, the elixir of everlasting life, the universal panacea, the magic mirror and magic wand. And you will find them by learning to work with the sephiroth: *Malkuth, Yesod, Tiphareth, Daath, and Kether.*

Chapter Six

AIN SOPH AUR

UNLIMITED LIGHT

When we open our window in the morning and get a glimpse of the sun, we are happy to see its light, feel its warmth, and let the life that pours from it soak into us. But if we could rise above the earth and go much closer to the sun, we might find something dark and obscure that would not make us happy at all—quite the contrary. There is a mystery here that needs to be considered more closely, for all those who have reached great heights in their quest for light have had an analogous experience. In fact, many have never been seen again, for when one has reached such heights one cannot return to earth. A moth is consumed by the flame of the lamp that attracts it. Those who have ventured to make contact with the Absolute have disappeared, dissolved by the force of its vibrations. This is why it is said that *Kether*, the highest sephirah, absorbs or pulverizes those who reach it.

This is the meaning of the Old Testament stories of the disappearance of Enoch, who 'walked with God; then he was no more, for God took him,' and of Elijah, who was carried off by a chariot of fire and horses of fire, and 'ascended in a whirlwind into heaven.' Fire consumes objects and transforms them into flame, and the same is true of light. Does this seem terrifying? No, to be absorbed by light, to melt away in that region that can be identified neither as light nor darkness, is the experience that all initiates long for above all others.

In ancient Egypt, when a disciple attained the highest degree of initiation, the high priest whispered in his ear: 'Osiris is a dark god... Osiris is darkness, three times darkness.' How could Osiris, the god of light and of the sun, be dark? The disciple was troubled by this, for darkness symbolizes evil and the unknowable. What bitterness to have sought light, to have run the full course, only to find that it ends in darkness! But the reality is that Osiris is so luminous that he seems dark. He is the light beyond light. Why do we speak of a 'blinding light'? There seems to be a contradiction here, but it is only apparent. On the physical plane, we do not say that something is light unless we can see it with our eyes. That which our eyes cannot see we call shadow or night, and even compared with certain animals that have night vision, our perception in this respect is relative. If nothing in your previous experience has prepared you to understand the thought of a very great philosopher or scientist, however much light it may shed on certain questions, many things will remain obscure for you. In fact, the more luminous their thought, the more obscure it will seem to those who are incapable of understanding it. In this context, the words 'darkness' and 'obscurity' are not intended to define an objective reality: only to express our inability to grasp it mentally. Whereas what we call light corresponds to a reality that is more accessible. This is why we can say that, for us, light always emerges from darkness.

This means that we shall never know whether darkness is truly dark, or whether it simply appears as darkness to us because of our inability to see. How can we know whether darkness is a reality or not? The initiates can help us to understand this: in their desire to instruct human beings in the mysteries of God and of creation, they teach that light is born of darkness. In the beginning of the Book of Genesis, for instance, it says: 'The earth was a formless void, and darkness covered the face of the deep, while a wind from God swept over the face of the waters. Then God said, "Let there be light;" and there was light.'

The world of the ten sephiroth that we are studying is the world of manifestation, the world as it has been from the moment God said: 'Let there be light.' But this does not mean that darkness reigned before that moment—on the contrary. This is why cabbalists designate the space beyond *Kether* as *Ain Soph Aur*, Unlimited Light. The region of *Ain Soph Aur* is like a veil that cannot be penetrated by human beings. It is the absolute, the unmanifest, of which we can have no notion, and of which *Kether*, God the Father, is an emanation.

The Deity, as conceived by the cabbalists, is beyond light and darkness, beyond the created worlds. In an attempt to express the mystery of the Godhead even more clearly, they conceived the notion of a region beyond *Ain Soph Aur*, which they called *Ain Soph*, Unlimited; and beyond that again, a region called *Ain*, Un, or negation. Thus at the origin of the universe there is a negation. But the Un that denotes absence or lack does not mean non-existence. *Ain* is not the absolute nothingness that some see in the Nirvana of Hinduism. It is, in fact, the exact opposite. *Ain Soph Aur*, like Nirvana, is not non-existence, not annihilation, but life beyond creation, beyond manifestation—so far beyond that it seems to us to be non-existence.

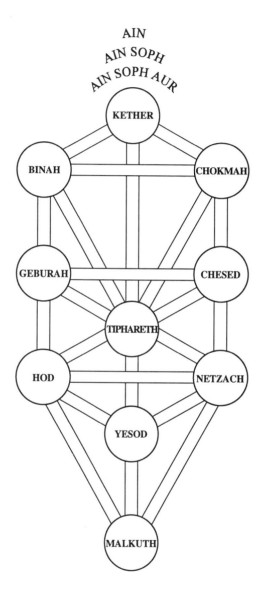

The Sephirotic Tree

Ain, Ain Soph, Ain Soph Aur are the terms that cabbalists use to express those realities that cannot be comprehended by the human mind. There is really nothing we can say about the Absolute. But try to hold on to these notions and thank God, your heavenly Father, for them. For the Father loves you, and works in your heart, and helps you to grow, and these words can, after all, help you to have some sense, however slight, of these realities. Ask heaven for the light you need to penetrate these mysteries. All I can do is point you in the right direction.

Chapter Seven

LIGHT

THE SUBSTANCE OF THE UNIVERSE

'Let there be light!' According to the Book of Genesis, creation began when God pronounced these words. Does this mean that no light existed before that? And how could the divine Word create light? Once more, the Tree of Life can help us to understand.

Before God said, 'Let there be light,' the reality that we call light existed only in a form that was inconceivable to us: that which is known as *Ain Soph Aur*. Also, the 'Word' of God has no connection with what we understand by a word. It is simply a way of expressing the notion that, in order to create, God projected something from himself. What he projected was himself, but a new form of himself: that which we call light. To say that God 'spoke' means that he willed to manifest himself. You are probably thinking that this is very difficult to understand. Not really. Let me illustrate it with an example from everyday life. Let us say that you have an idea. Yes, but where is that idea? Can you place it? Can you see it or find it in a particular spot in your brain? No. And you also have to admit that you do not know exactly what kind of matter it is made of. But as soon as you express that idea in words its existence becomes perceptible. And when you eventually put your idea into effect it is actualized and can be perceived. A word is the intermediary between the plane of thought and that of material reality. And this gives you an idea of the process of creation.

Now, if we put this phrase from Genesis, 'In the beginning... God said, "Let there be light",' side by side with the opening words of St John's Gospel, 'In the beginning was the Word, and the Word was with God, and the Word was God,' it will help us to understand better the relationship between the Word and light. Light is the substance that the divine Word, the first-born of God, brought forth to serve as the matter of creation. You will say that when you look at stones, plants, animals, and even human beings you cannot see that they are made of light. True, but that is because the light they are made of has been condensed to such a degree that it has become opaque. The very fact that we generally envisage light as being opposed to matter shows that we do not realize that what we call matter is actually condensed light.

The Cabbalah teaches that God created the world by a process of successive condensations. In order to emerge from that immensity, that unfathomable abyss, that infinite space in which he dwelt, *Ain Soph Aur*, the Absolute, the Unknowable, imposed limits on himself, and then, overflowing those limits, he formed a receptacle, which he filled with his emanations. This receptacle is *Kether*, the first sephirah. *Kether* is the first manifestation of *Ain Soph Aur*, the unmanifest. Thus one can say that the whole of creation is simply a successive process of the original light pouring out and overflowing from one vessel to the next. *Kether* overflows and forms *Chokmah; Chokmah* is, as it were, a vessel filled with the waters of *Kether. Chokmah* overflows into *Binah; Binah* into *Chesed; Chesed* into *Geburah. Geburah* overflows into *Tiphareth; Tiphareth* into *Netzach; Netzach* into *Hod; Hod* into *Yesod,* and *Yesod* into *Malkuth.* And as the divine emanation works its way downwards to form new worlds, it becomes more and more dense. But it is always the same quintessence that ceaselessly creates new forces, new colours, new melodies, new forms. From emanation to emanation God created the sephiroth, and life continues to flow from the infinite source.

'In the beginning was the Word, and the Word was with God, and the Word was God... In him was life, and the life was the light of all people.' In order for *Kether* to pour forth life, it had to receive it from above, and it received it from *Ain Soph Aur*. *Ain Soph Aur* received it from *Ain Soph*, and *Ain Soph* received it from *Ain,* the absence that was awaiting the moment to become presence.

There is, therefore, an unbroken association between the Absolute and the manifest God, and it is thus that something new is continually being introduced into the universe. The universe is a continuous creation, the matter of which constantly increases and is transformed. How is this relationship between the Absolute and God established? We do not know. Indeed, may God forgive me for intruding into such questions, for we must have the courage to confess that nobody knows anything about this. Why talk about it then? Because, insofar as we are created in the image of God, in the image of the universe, something in us that is beyond the realm of consciousness can grasp some tiny particles of this reality.

Life is simply a decantation of energies. This is why we find in the cabbalistic tradition the image of the river of life that flows from the divine source and waters all the regions of the universe.

From *Kether* to *Malkuth*, the sephiroth are sacred vessels filled by the inexhaustible source of life. Two complementary images, that of a tree and that of a river, illustrate the outpouring and flow of life. You will say that the roots of a tree are down below, whereas the source of a river is up above. Yes, in our material world the roots of trees are in the ground, but the roots of the cosmic tree are in the world above.[1]

Now, let us take the image of a river, bearing in mind that it is no more than that: an image that illustrates one aspect of reality. But as reality itself is far more complex, we need to introduce other elements in order to understand it.

Since the sephiroth are situated on three pillars, it follows that the river of life does not flow in a straight line from top to bottom. As we have seen, on each side of the central pillar are the Pillar of Mercy, polarized positively, and the Pillar of Severity, polarized negatively. As it flows from one sephirah to the next, therefore, the polarization of the divine emanation changes, and the sephiroth, following on one from another, appear to be in

---

[1]   See chapter 9 of this volume.

opposition with the one before and the one after. *Chokmah*, for example, which represents harmony and universal love, is followed by *Binah*, which represents the implacable rigour of divine decrees. Following on the intransigence of *Binah*, comes the clemency of *Chesed,* followed in turn by the martial audacity of *Geburah*, and so on. And as each sephirah corresponds to a divine attribute, a divine virtue, the adjectives used to describe God are not only very different, but they also seem to be contradictory: merciful and terrible, tender and jealous, faithful and vengeful, and so on. All these epithets express the starkly opposite character of the two pillars.

Chapter Eight

'WHEN GOD DREW A CIRCLE

ON THE FACE OF THE DEEP'

When God wants to descend into our world, he has to clothe himself just as we do. And to clothe oneself means to descend to the material plane. But as God does not want to assume all the limitations of a physical body in order to be with us, he invites us to his own home. And his home is also ours. Yes, our home is immense, infinitely bigger than we imagine. Our home is the universe that God fills, impregnates, and sustains with his presence, and it is by journeying through that universe that we can be with God.

When I speak of journeying through the universe it is not a question simply of exploring it with rockets and spacecraft. It is a question of using all the means that the Creator has given us in order to study it; of using our physical sense organs, of course, but also, and especially, the organs of our spiritual senses, our soul and spirit. This is the only way to meet the Lord. He will not descend any further to be with us. He has already imposed the limits of creation on himself. He will not limit himself more than this.

You will be thinking: 'But God is absolutely free. What does it mean to say that he has limited himself?' Let me explain.

The sephiroth *Kether*, *Chokmah*, and *Binah* correspond to the entity that Christians call God.[1] *Kether*, *Chokmah*, and *Binah* represent the Holy Trinity, one God in three persons. It is this Trinity (which the Cabbalah situates on the plane of emanations, *Atziluth*) that created and continues to be present in the world.

The first sephirah, *Kether*, represents the beginning of all manifestation and is thus identified with the Father. And *Kether* engenders *Chokmah*. What is *Chokmah*? It is the Logos, the divine Word, an energy that is condensed and organized in order to become the matter of creation. This is why St John wrote: 'In the beginning was the Word.'

Now, imagine for a moment that you want to invent a new way of expressing yourself, so you create the equivalent of an alphabet: this cosmic alphabet is *Chokmah*. And now that you have the letters of your alphabet, you can juggle with them and organize them to form words

---

[1] See Chapter 10 of this volume, *The Cosmic Family and the Mystery of the Trinity.*

and rational, intelligible sentences. This third phase is *Binah*, primordial matter. Primordial matter must be understood to mean essences, not the material elements that are familiar to us and the objects of scientific study. This primordial substance that comes from *Chokmah* is differentiated in *Binah*, and it is only after a very lengthy process of condensation that it begins to appear on the physical plane in the form of the elements that we call oxygen, hydrogen, iron, zinc, and so on. The elements of the Logos—letters and numbers—grouped into sentences are the archetypes of material bodies, and their properties are fixed and unchangeable.[2] To each element the third sephirah, *Binah,* has assigned its proper place, composition, weight, and properties.

The sephirah *Kether* is beyond time and space. Space first appears with *Chokmah* and is represented on the material plane by *Mazloth*, the zodiac; time first appears with *Binah*, in the form of *Shabbathai*, Saturn. When God—that is, the Trinity of *Kether-Chokmah-Binah*—withdraws, there will be no more time or space and the universe will disappear. When the sacrifice implicit in God's

---

[2] There is no written form for numbers in Hebrew, but the letters of the alphabet have numerical value, thus,, א (aleph) = 1, ב (bet) =2, ג (gimmel) = 3, and so on.

limitation on himself ceases, the created world will return to nothingness, but from this nothingness a new creation will come forth, of which we know nothing.

Nothing is eternal except God himself, and one day the whole of creation will go back into God. But what exactly do we mean by this word 'creation'? If you consider that it refers to the primordial matter that emanated from God, then the elements that constitute this matter are indestructible: they remain forever in God and it is with them that he will always be able to engender new worlds. But if you say that 'creation' means the worlds that God formed out of those elements, then it is not eternal. All that is born must die. Eternity is not a succession of centuries. It is very difficult to define such a notion, but you might say that eternity is, as it were, a quality of matter, a fusion of matter and spirit. When we experience eternity, it is as a sensation that we experience it. And if it is possible for us to have a sensation of eternity—if only for a few seconds—it is because we have entered a higher order of being, we have been projected into a world in which matter is animated by the most intense vibrations of the spirit.

Primordial matter is the substance that God projected from himself and condensed. It alone is indestructible and eternal. It is with this matter that God created the worlds, and one day these worlds will disintegrate before reappearing in new forms. It is in this sense that we can say that creation will come to an end.

'Heaven and earth will pass away, but my words will not pass away,' said Jesus. When he expressed himself in this way, Jesus was identifying with the second person of the Trinity, the Son, the second sephirah, *Chokmah*, the Logos. Heaven and earth will pass away, that is true, but the seeds that are in *Chokmah* are the archetypes for a new heaven and a new earth, and they will not pass away, for they are eternal.

'When God drew a circle on the face of the deep, I was there,' says *Chokmah*, Wisdom, in the Book of Proverbs. What was this circle? It was the boundary, the outer limits drawn by God when he created the world. It is in this sense that we can say that God limited himself. To limit oneself means to enclose oneself in a universe that functions and evolves according to its own laws. We do not know what exists outside or beyond those limits. The laws of life studied by science are simply the limits that God imposed upon himself in his creation. It is these limits that give structure, form, shape, and cohesion to matter. A world that was not circumscribed by limits would be unstable. It could not endure, for all the matter within those limits is in motion, perpetually seeking to burst its bonds.

God drew a circle in order to restrain his own substance. The circle is a magical outline. In the centre of this circle God placed the seed of creation, and his work began. Everything in nature reveals the way in which God created the world. A single cell with its surrounding membrane tells us the whole story. If our skull did not exist, where would our brain be? And the skin, too, serves as a limit; this is its function. Observe the things around you: wherever you look you will see a reflection of the circle that God drew in order to circumscribe his creation. If you do not put perfume in a closed bottle it evaporates. And the same goes for a house: you have to begin by fixing the outer perimeter. If there were no outside walls where would your house be? Even in the spiritual domain we have to understand how this question of limits applies. A magus draws a circle round himself before convoking spirits of light to help him in his work; and all disciples should know that, if only through thought, they must draw a circle of light around themselves so as to preserve their spiritual energies.

God exists in all aspects of creation, from the stones—in which he is most severely restricted and in which we can even touch him—to the most immaterial of substances, light, and beyond. He is omnipresent: in stones, plants, animals, human beings, the angels, and all the celestial hierarchies. His members are deeply embedded in every area of creation, but in some regions he is freer than in others. In the denser forms of matter he is not free to move, but in his kingdom he is free. If you understand this, many windows will open before you to reveal glorious horizons.

God is free, yes, but he is free only outside our world. Once he enters our world he finds himself restricted. This is why, when people are scandalized by certain events and cry out against God, saying that he should not allow such things, it shows that they simply do not understand. If they possessed true knowledge, they would realize that God cannot intervene. God's freedom of action on earth is limited; and it is we who limit it. God is free and at the same time he is not free; he is not free in our hearts, but he is free in the hearts of the angels.

Let me illustrate this. Imagine someone who amuses himself by cementing one of his feet to the ground: he will be unable to move that foot, but all the rest of his body will be free. Similarly, God allows himself to be imprisoned in the cement of humanity, but only partially. The day God frees himself completely and withdraws his foot from the cement, there will be no more humanity. This is only an image, of course, but it can help you to understand better the reality of things.

In order to manifest himself, God is willing to restrict himself. We can go even further: we can say that it is thanks to that restriction that we exist and are able to think of him and talk about him. It is God himself who gives us this possibility. The proof that God exists is the fact that I am here talking to you about him, and that you are there listening to me. If he did not exist, I should not exist, and neither would you. Everything that exists is proof of the existence of God. Of course, if people prefer to have a different idea of God, so as to be able to say that he does not exist—or that he is dead—well that is their business.

Jesus said: 'You are the temple of the living God.' This God of whom we are the temple is the God that is manifest, and the degree to which his freedom is restricted in us depends on our degree of evolution. As we rise gradually to a higher plane and become progressively purer, we gradually liberate God and make it possible for him to manifest himself more freely in our temple, in the form of power, light, love, and beauty.

Of course, all these ideas are difficult to grasp, and you will soon forget them again, I know. But some trace of them will remain in your subconscious, and, one day when you are capable of understanding, you will remember them again. If you want to accelerate this process of understanding, you must train your brain, which is the best of instruments. It does not deteriorate at the same rate as your other organs because the divine hierarchies have placed their powers in it, but it needs to be exercised by the activity of thought. Thought is a kind of ladder that we have received from cosmic intelligence, and it is essential to learn to use it to rise to greater heights.

Chapter Nine

THE KINGDOM OF GOD

IS LIKE A MUSTARD SEED

To say that God is absolutely unknowable is false. A being whose works can be contemplated night and day is not wholly unknowable. The universe created by God exists and is at least partly accessible to our five senses and our faculties of thought, and this means that God, too, is partly accessible to us. True, beyond *Kether* God is totally out of our reach, but with *Kether* we enter a region in which it is possible for us to grasp certain notions.

Kether, the first sephirah, represents the beginning of all manifestation, and manifestation implies division and polarization, the appearance, that is, of the masculine and feminine principles necessary for creation.

Perhaps the image of a seed will help to understand this idea. As long as a seed has not 'manifested' itself, we cannot know anything about it. The life within it is immobile. But if you plant it and water it, it divides and produces a tiny shoot which grows into a stem and appears above ground. Only then can you begin to know it. God has left clues, traces of himself, throughout nature for our instruction. If God, the undivided, unpolarized Absolute who contains all that is, had not become polarized in order to manifest himself, we would not exist, and would not, therefore, know anything about him, just as we know nothing about a seed until it sprouts, until it is polarized.

The image of the seed is precisely the one Jesus uses in the parable:

> *The kingdom of heaven is like a mustard seed that someone took and sowed in his field; it is the smallest of all the seeds, but when it has grown it is the greatest of shrubs and becomes a tree, so that the birds of the air come and make nests in its branches.*

The kingdom of God is the universe, of which the Sephirotic Tree, or Tree of Life, is one of its most profound symbolic representations.

Look! The sower plants the seed in the ground, and this is the first sephirah, *Kether*. The life process cannot start until the seed is planted.

Once in the ground, the seed divides, that is, it polarizes and produces *Chokmah*, Wisdom, duality, the opposition of positive and negative, of higher and lower. The forces dormant in the Crown (*Kether*) begin to divide and oppose one another. And this explains why those who cannot understand duality, oppositions, good and evil, cannot understand wisdom.

In reality these forces are not completely separated; they are still linked by the Crown, which tells them: 'You are masculine and feminine, positive and negative, and you must now unite and go and work together in the world.' Then these forces unite, and this is *Binah*, Understanding, in which they are harmonized. As commanded by the Crown, *Binah* reconciles the contradictory forces, and the seed sprouts.

Kether, *Chokmah*, and *Binah* are the roots planted in the soil of the higher world. You will say that the roots of a plant are supposed to be down below, in the ground. Yes, but this is because the roots of a plant represent the head. The true head is above. Human beings, too, are trees whose roots are planted in the world above, in heaven. Our true head, just like *Kether*, *Chokmah*, and *Binah*, is buried in the soil of the divine world.

Now, in order for the plant to appear above ground, the intervention of the fourth sephirah—*Chesed,* Mercy—is necessary. *Chesed* represents the trunk of the tree, the force that stands up against every adversity.

The fifth sephirah—*Geburah,* Strength—corresponds to the branches that begin to spread in all directions. When human beings, societies, or nations become very powerful they are able to spread far and wide.

The sixth sephirah—*Tiphareth*, Beauty—represents the leaves, which not only clothe the tree, but also enable it to breathe and be nourished by light.

After the leaves come the buds, and this is the seventh sephirah—*Netzach,* Victory. The fact that the tree has reached the stage of producing buds means that it has been capable of overcoming all difficulties and is ready to produce fruit.

At this stage a great deal of work is going on in the buds which are going to give birth to flowers. This is the eighth sephirah—*Hod*, Glory, Praise. The tree is covered with flowers, whose perfume rises like incense as an offering to celebrate the glory of the everlasting Lord.

Finally, within the flower a fruit is formed, which is brought to maturity and given colour by the sun. This is the formation of the child, the ninth sephirah—*Yesod*, Foundation—and this fruit will be the starting point of another life, a new tree.

The fruit that has grown from the first seed itself contains seeds, and these seeds are *Malkuth*, the tenth sephirah. Originally one, the seed has now become ten, that is, symbolically speaking, a multitude. Every seed produced by the fruit represents *Malkuth*, the Kingdom of God. How can we tell that it is truly the Kingdom of God? You only have to plant the seed and before long all the other attributes will manifest themselves. Thus *Malkuth* and *Kether* come together; the beginning and the end are identical. This is why Jesus said that the Kingdom of God (*Malkuth*) was like a mustard seed.

Now you are perhaps thinking: 'All that is very nice, but how can we possibly make use of it for our inner life?' In many ways. The mustard seed can be understood as a thought or a feeling. What is a thought or a feeling? It is a seed, which, at first sight, seems minute. But plant it, and if it is pure, unselfish, and intense, and if you provide good conditions in which it can grow, it will be the starting point for the edification of the Kingdom of God. 'The birds of the air will come and make nests in its branches,' said Jesus. The 'birds of the air' are the angels, for those who have embraced the spiritual life are always visited by angels who come and take shelter and make their permanent abode within them, and fill them with their light and their gifts.

It is said that God created man in his image and likeness. What does this mean? You will begin to understand when you have meditated for a long time on the notion of the seed and the tree. The whole question of the 'image and likeness' is contained in the distance that lies between the seed and the tree.

Chapter Ten

THE COSMIC FAMILY

AND

THE MYSTERY OF THE TRINITY

There is nothing in the visible world that is not a reflection, a representation of the invisible world. Take the example of the family: the family, consisting basically of father, mother, son and daughter, is a reality on earth, and seeing it, we are meant to understand that the family also exists on the highest plane—although on that plane it exists in the form of cosmic principles at work in the universe.

These cosmic principles are represented by the sacred name of God, Yod He Vau He יהוה, which, in the cabbalistic tradition, is also known as the *Tetragrammaton* (from the Greek *tetra*, meaning four, and *gramma*, meaning letter). The four letters of the name of God correspond to the four principles at work in the universe, and these four principles are also at work in human beings, for human beings were created in the image of the universe.

Yod ' is the creative masculine principle, the primordial force that is at the origin of all movement: the spirit, the father.

Heh ה represents the feminine principle, which absorbs, preserves, protects, and allows the creative principle to work within her. This is the soul, the mother.

Vau ו represents the son that is born of the union of father and mother. It is the first-born of this union, and it, too, manifests itself as an active principle, although on a different level. The son is the intellect that follows the direction laid down by the father. This characteristic of Vau is represented graphically in its written form, which is a prolonged version of Yod.

The second Heh ה represents the daughter. The daughter is a repetition of the mother. This is the heart.

Thus the four letters of the name of God represent the father, the spirit; the mother, the soul; the son, the intellect, and the daughter, the heart.

On the Tree of Life these four principles correspond to the first four sephiroth: *Kether* is the father; *Chokmah* the son, and *Binah* the daughter. 'And what about the mother?' you will ask. The mother corresponds to the sephirah *Daath*.[1]   This is the divine Mother who is also known to cabbalists as *Shekinah*, the Bride of God. Oh yes—I ask Christians to forgive me and not to be scandalized—but God does have a bride, a spouse! I, too, am a Christian, but I cannot see that that is any reason to refuse to think and try to understand things as they really are.

I have no intention—any more than the cabbalists—of attributing to God a spouse in the sense in which a man has a spouse, a wife, on earth. But insofar as the family is a reality below, it is also a reality above. Of course, it is a reality that manifests itself very differently. It is a question of analogy, not of identity. The Emerald Tablet of Hermes Trismegistus says: 'That which is below is *like* that which is above, and that which is above is *like* that which is below.' It is quite clear, therefore, that it is an analogy, not an exact resemblance.

Christians talk about Father, Son, and Holy Ghost, and they never seem to be surprised that there is no mention of a feminine principle. And yet, how can one avoid asking oneself the question? When you hear the words 'father and son', which evoke the notion of family, how can you fail to be surprised that the third member of this family is not the mother but the

---

[1]   See chapter 3.

Holy Ghost? What kind of family can there be
with the absence of a mother? But in this
family she is absent; she has been replaced by
the Holy Ghost. Why? Ah, that is something
you are going to have to ask the Fathers of the
Church: why they made the Lord out to be a
confirmed bachelor! The three entities of this
Trinity—Father, Son, and Holy Ghost—are all
masculine, and it is not normal that there
should be no place for the feminine principle.
For, as you well understand, it is a question of
principles.

It was because they had eliminated the
divine Mother as a cosmic principle that
Christian theologians later gave so much
importance to Mary, the mother of Jesus
(actually, it is possible that the black Madonnas
found in certain churches may be vestiges of a
belief in the cosmic Mother). Mary was given
too prominent a place and believed to have
virtues and powers that no woman can possess.
She was declared to be the 'Immaculate
Conception', which means that from the
moment of her conception she was preserved
from the stain of original sin. And she herself
was said to have conceived Jesus 'through the
operation of the Holy Spirit.' I have no
objection to all this. If it gives people pleasure
to believe these things about the mother of
Jesus, let them do so, by all means. However, I

am obliged to recognize that these beliefs contradict all the laws of nature established by cosmic intelligence. However great and exalted in character, however divine a human being may be, he cannot be physically conceived by the Holy Ghost.

How is it possible to confuse Mary and the divine Mother? I have great regard and esteem for Mary and no desire to belittle her, but still, you cannot make her out to be the divine Mother! Christians have no understanding of the immensity of this cosmic principle, which is the feminine dimension of the creative principle. The being that we call God, and that Christianity sees as a masculine force, is in reality both masculine and feminine. Before there can be creation, manifestation, there has to be polarization, that is, the presence of a masculine principle and a feminine principle. In order to manifest himself, God has to be both masculine and feminine. This is what was taught already in Orphic initiation: God is both male and female.

Why did the Fathers of the Church do away with the divine Mother? Were they so puritanical that the idea of God having a spouse shocked them? The true reason, no doubt, is that, having identified Jesus with the Christ to the point of claiming that he was truly the only begotten Son of God who had come to

incarnate in this world, they had to give him a
mother with as little that was human in her as
possible. Thus they identified Mary with the
divine Mother, just as they had identified Jesus
with the Christ. Here again, they are free to
believe what they like, but is it the truth? Mary
was a woman, she is not the divine Mother who
formed the worlds. Mary is not the Mother of
God: she was the mother of Jesus. And Jesus is
not a cosmic principle: Jesus was a man, one of
the greatest of the sons of God born on earth,
but still a man. And the Christ is the cosmic
principle who came to dwell in him. Why
confuse everything? Of course, the fact that
heaven chose Mary to be the mother of such a
being as Jesus shows that she must have been
an exceptional woman. But that does not justify
putting her in the place of the divine Mother.

The four letters of the name of God, Yod
He Vau He יהוה, represent, therefore, the four
principles that are at the origin of creation: the
heavenly Father and the divine Mother, who
find their prolongation in the son and daughter.
Thus, on the Sephirotic Tree we have *Kether*,
the father; *Daath*, the mother; *Chokmah*, the
son, and *Binah*, nature, the daughter.

Perhaps you will ask whether this means
that you should discard the notion of the
Trinity, Father, Son, and Holy Ghost. No, but
you have to understand what these three

principles correspond to. Christianity defines the Holy Trinity as the mystery of one God in three persons. But the Trinity is not a mystery; or, rather, it is a mystery only because nobody has known how to apply the law of analogy to it. In order to understand what I mean we have to call upon the sun.

The sun is that extraordinarily powerful life-creating force that manifests itself through light and love. Those who are capable of a profound understanding of these manifestations will soon discover the relationships that exist between the life, light, and warmth of the sun on the one hand, and the Trinity, Father-Son-Holy Spirit on the other. On every plane of creation, from the physical to the divine, these three principles—life, light, and warmth—are present. On the spiritual plane, life manifests itself as wisdom (light) and love (warmth), and it is these three principles—life, light, and warmth—that we find again in the Trinity. Father, Son, and Holy Spirit are indissolubly united, just as the life, light, and warmth of the sun are indissolubly united. As you see, the mystery of one God in three persons is not really so difficult to understand. The only thing that remains a mystery is the immensity and splendour of that primordial essence from which came all forms of existence. On this we must never cease to meditate.

Thus the Holy Trinity is represented on the Sephirotic Tree by the three sephiroth *Kether*, *Chokmah*, and *Binah*. When we pronounce the word 'God', we must realize that we are actually touching these first three sephiroth. 'What exactly is the relationship between them and the Trinity?' you will ask. 'Can we say that they correspond?' Yes, on condition that you know how to handle these correspondences delicately and with intelligence.

Kether, the Crown, represents the Father, source of all life. This correspondence is quite clear; it presents no difficulty.

The second sephirah, *Chokmah*, issues from the Father, and can be seen to correspond to the Son, the divine Word uttered by the Father, the light that he projected from himself in the act of creation.

The third sephirah, *Binah*, corresponds to the Holy Spirit, who is thus considered to be a feminine power. Many people will be indignant at the idea of considering the Holy Spirit to be a 'woman'. But I said nothing about a 'woman'; I spoke only of a feminine power, a feminine principle. Besides, what is there to be indignant about? Were you scandalized when the Holy Spirit was represented as a dove? What else is a dove but a bird to which are attributed feminine characteristics? Besides, in the New Testament, the Holy Spirit is called the 'Paraclete', a Greek word that means one who helps, protects, and consoles, one who is an expression of love and warmth. Ah yes, we need to enlarge our understanding!

Now, as I have explained in previous talks,[2] there is nothing absolute about these correspondences. You can equally well consider that the Son represents love, since it is he who offers himself as an eternal sacrifice for the preservation of the world. And the Holy Spirit can be seen as representing wisdom, since it was the Spirit that descended on the apostles in the form of tongues of fire, and gave them the gifts of prophecy and tongues. It was also to the Holy Spirit that Jesus referred when he spoke to his disciples just before leaving them: 'I still have many things to say to you, but you cannot bear them now. When the Spirit of truth comes, will guide you into all the truth.' The only point that is hard and fast is that *Kether* represents the Father, life, with his two manifestations, light and heat, which, on this plane just as on the physical plane, can be transformed one into the other.

And now, if you are willing to persevere in your efforts and come even further with me, I will add that according to a cabbalistic tradition *Chokmah*, Wisdom, is the feminine principle

---

[2] See *The Splendour of Tiphareth*, vol. 10 of the Complete Works, particularly chapters 4 and 10.

that is identified with the *Shekinah*, the spouse of God. This means that *Chokmah* represents the divine Mother. 'In this case, where is the Son?' you will ask. The Son is one with the Mother, they are inseparable. How can one speak of a mother without thinking of her son, and how can one speak of a son without thinking of his mother? One sees this idea represented in certain paintings of the Virgin and Child. Many painters have portrayed Mary holding Jesus in her arms or on her knees. The child is in the centre, and depending on how you look at the picture, you can either look at him alone, or at him and his mother as an undivided whole. But even if you focus only on the child, his mother is always there.

When you adopt these correspondences—*Kether* being the Father, *Chokmah* being Mother and Son—you find the Daughter in *Binah*, and the whole family is there once more. You will say that the whole thing is quite incomprehensible! On the contrary, nothing could be clearer or more precise! This is the living Cabbalah. The only thing is that you cannot enter these realms unless your mind is free and unencumbered. Only on that condition will there always be new treasures for you to discover and understand.

It is very important to understand the meaning of the Trinity in the light of the

Cabbalah. But it is even more important to learn to be in communion with it every day through the life, light, and warmth of the sun. This is a law that I shall never tire of repeating, for it is an essential foundation of the spiritual life: all that exists down here in our physical world reflects what exists above in the divine world. The Holy Trinity is not in the light, or the heat, or even in the life of the star that we call the sun; it is far beyond these physical realities. But through that light, heat, and life we can come closer to it, we can be in communion with it, we can invite it into ourselves and thus receive its blessings.

Chapter Eleven

THE BODY OF ADAM KADMON

The Tree of Life is the universe in which God dwells and which is impregnated with his life. It represents the divine life that flows throughout creation. And human beings, who were created in the image of God, are also an image of the universe. Of course, when one sees how most human beings behave, one cannot help thinking that they do not reflect a very glorious image. True, a human being seems to be nothing at all, and yet he is the whole universe, he is God.

Human intelligence is only capable of comprehending a three-dimensional world; it cannot grasp all the aspects of a human being. What we can see, touch, and hear is only a very small part of the reality. We do not know the true person, only his outer wrappings. Like a deep-sea diver in his diving suit, or an Eskimo swathed to the eyes in furs, a human being is enveloped in several layers, and it is these that we know a little about. If we were capable of stripping away these layers one after the other, we should discover that they conceal a minute point, an atom of light. And yet, we know that a human being is truly immense, that he embraces the whole universe. These two statements are simultaneously true, and the symbol of this truth is the circle with a point in the centre, the symbol of the sun: the infinitely small point that has no dimension, and the infinitely vast circle that embraces and unifies all that is. It is up to us now to seek out the true human being that dwells in each one of us, the being that was created in the image of God.

When the Cabbalah speaks of the creation of man, it is not speaking of human beings as they are today. It is speaking about Adam Kadmon, whose name means 'primordial man' (Adam, man, and Kadmon, primordial). Adam Kadmon is the cosmic man. His body is formed by the constellations and worlds. He is the first being created by God. God is beyond the created universe, beyond the sephirah, *Kether*; and Adam begins in *Kether*; *Kether* is the head of Adam Kadmon. *Chokmah* is his right eye and the right side of his face; *Binah* is his left eye and the left side of his face. *Chesed* is his right arm; *Geburah* the left; *Tiphareth* the heart and solar plexus; *Netzach* the right leg; *Hod* the left leg; *Yesod* his sexual organs, and *Malkuth*

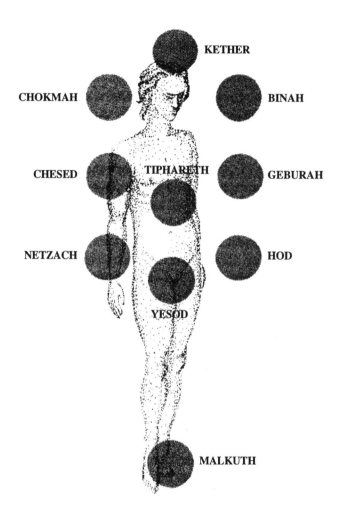

Adam Kadmon

his feet. Adam Kadmon is the archetype of which we are a cell, a reflection.

I could draw a parallel between Adam Kadmon and the entity whom Christians call the Christ, which would show you how they relate to each other, but I hesitate to do so, for fear of upsetting you.

Whatever we can say about man is only an approximation of the truth, just as it is for God. This is why we are obliged to have recourse to images, symbols, and analogies. It is by studying the Sephirotic Tree, which is a reflection of the universe, that we can begin to understand the true dimensions of man. Conversely, one can have some idea of the universe if one understands that man was created in its image. In other words, by studying man, his nature and his functions, we shall get to know the universe, because all that is in the universe is reflected in man. To find the answer to even the most abstract philosophical questions, all you need to do is observe man.

Man is a key. Even his physical form is that of a key: ♀. Why did the ancient Egyptians represent their hierophants holding a key? Because that key sums up the whole of man; this is the key that enables an initiate to unlock the fifty gates of *Binah*, the cosmic Mother, primordial matter. To say that those who hold this key can open the fifty gates means that they know all the properties of numbers and entities and all the relationships that can be established between them. Once they have discovered within themselves the key that opens all doors, they can go up and down on the cosmic ladder, and all the wealth of the universe created by God is at their disposal.

Whatever their degree of evolution, all human beings, created in the image of God, are inhabited by a higher soul that reaches to heaven, which is an emanation of God. This is why your life will have real meaning only when you are in touch with that immortal soul that is light, harmony, and power. It is through this soul that you can be in communion both with the Creator and with the universe that he created, for it is in itself the quintessence of that universe. And if you think of it and have recourse to it more often, if you link yourself to it, if you speak to it and identify with it, you will begin to understand what your true self really is. Then your consciousness will reach a higher plane, and its vibrations will become ever more intense until it melts into the consciousness of that sublime, higher soul, and you become one with God.

Man has his origin in God; it is God who acts and works through him. And one day he will return to God; he will cease to exist as a personal entity and will melt back into God. Of course, I know that this idea does not please many people, because they see it as a threat to their individual freedom. But, whether they like it or not, this is the reality. So, as often as possible, instead of wasting your time in futile occupations, instead of brooding on all the things that worry or hurt you, occupy your minds by thinking of that soul that is you, even if it is not completely you yet, because you still do not know how to join up with it. If you do this often you will gradually feel peace and joy, particularly joy, filling you to overflowing.

From the stones and plants all the way to the archangels and to God, all that has existence in the universe exists also in man. All the elements of creation are present even in our physical body. Nothing is missing, and this is why there are no bounds to the progress we can make. We can continue to advance indefinitely. But in order to do so we have to work on our own matter so as to make it so flexible and transparent, so vibrant, that it becomes capable of expressing the divine world. In this way we shall be able one day to manifest ourselves in all the fullness of our being as we are on high.

But we need a method to guide us in the spiritual life and show us the path to follow. And for me, as I have said, this method is the Sephirotic Tree. This is why I continue to urge you to study and become familiar with all its aspects. With *Malkuth* you materialize things. With *Yesod* you purify them. With *Hod* you understand and express them. With *Netzach* you imbue them with grace. With *Tiphareth* you illuminate them. With *Geburah* you fight to defend them. With *Chesed* you impose divine order on them. With *Binah* you give them stability. With *Chokmah* you integrate them into the universal harmony. Finally, with *Kether* you put the seal of eternity on them.

Learn to meditate on the ten sephiroth in the awareness that the Tree of Life is within you, and that the only worthwhile activity is to make it grow, and flower, and bear fruit. How many years—how many incarnations even—will it take for each one of you to become really and truly the Tree of Life? The answer does not matter. You may have to come back thousands of times before the ten sephiroth that are etched into your being begin to vibrate, and your inner being is illuminated by all the lights of the Tree of Life.

Chapter Twelve

MALKUTH, YESOD, HOD, TIPHARETH, ARCHANGELS AND SEASONS

The passage from one season to the next in the course of a year happens, as you know, when the sun passes through one of the four cardinal points known as solstices and equinoxes. Each of these points is a nexus of cosmic forces, and at these moments a flood of new energies pours into the earth. But the fact that this renewal occurs regularly does not mean that it is automatic or mechanical. No, all these changes are produced by the work of entities who have been entrusted with the care of stones, plants, animals, and human beings. Each of the four seasons comes under the influence of one of four archangels: *Raphaël* rules the spring; *Uriel* rules the summer; *Mikhaël* the autumn; and *Gabriel* the winter. Tradition tells us that *Raphaël*, *Uriel*, *Mikhaël*, and *Gabriel* are four of the seven spirits that are ever before the throne of God.

At the approach of the spring equinox, all the spirits and forces of nature set to work under the leadership of *Raphaël* to renew life in every region of the universe. The most spectacular results of their work can be seen in the vegetable kingdom, but it also influences minerals, animals, and human beings. This renewal of life in nature can be said to be synonymous with regeneration, and thus with healing, in human beings.

The only time *Raphaël* is mentioned in the Bible is in the marvellous story related in the Book of Tobias.[1]   One day, a blind old man called Tobit received a visit from a young man who introduced himself as Azariah, the son of one of Tobit's relations. Azariah suggested that he might accompany Tobit's son Tobias into Media, there to collect a sum of money that Tobit had left in trust with a friend twenty years before. Tobit accepted his proposal, and the two young men set out. On their way, Azariah instructed Tobias about many things and gave him much good advice. He even went so far as to suggest that Tobias ask for the hand in marriage of Sarah, the daughter of a man who had given them hospitality. However, the unfortunate Sarah was accursed: she had been married seven times, and each time a devil

---

[1] The Book of Tobias is one of the apocryphal books included in the Roman Catholic, Greek, and Slavonic Bibles.

called Asmodeus had killed her husband. In order to neutralize the curse, Azariah told Tobias to catch a particular kind of fish and to burn its heart and liver. The smoke from the burning fish would drive Asmodeus away. Tobias duly married Sarah, escaping the evil intentions of the demon Asmodeus, and went on his way. Tobit's money was eventually retrieved, and the party turned home. On the way, Azariah promised Tobias that he could heal his father's eyes by applying the gall of the fish, which would enable him to remove a little white skin from the eyes. Tobias does what Azariah prescribes and his father's sight is restored. At the end, when Tobias and his father want to give something to this extraordinary young man who had brought them such blessings, he at last revealed his true identity: 'I am *Raphaël*, one of the seven angels who stand ready and enter before the glory of the Lord.' What I have given you is only a brief summary, but the whole story is very beautiful and well worth reading.

According to cabbalists, the planet Mercury belongs in the sphere of *Hod*. Mercury (known as Hermes in Greek mythology) is the god of travellers and of health, and this is exactly the role played by *Raphaël* as he accompanied Tobias on his journey, instructing him in the art of healing the ills of the body (his father's blindness) and of the soul (the threats of the demon Asmodeus). It is not by chance that even in our times doctors use the symbol of the caduceus of Hermes.

The major feast day of spring is Easter, which celebrates the resurrection of Christ throughout the whole of nature, and which must be our resurrection too. It is not enough that we notice that the birds are singing again and the trees are covered with leaves; we have important work to do, a work of renewal. Every morning, when you come up to the sunrise, you should have only this renewal in mind, nothing else. Leave aside everything else, all that is old and obsolete, and open yourselves to this new life, so that you may enter into communion at last with this great tide flowing from the heart of the universe.

The summer is under the aegis of *Uriel*, a magnificent name which means God is my Light. There is no mention of this archangel in the Bible. In summer the whole of nature is aflame; the very air is on fire. 24 June is the feast of St John the Baptist, which coincides with the summer solstice, and it is the tradition on this night to light bonfires, and to celebrate the victory of heat and light by dancing and singing. However, the Church has never encouraged this way of celebrating the feast of St John, for it is all too reminiscent of the old pagan rites. Midnight celebrations that bring men and women to dance round a fire, singing and drinking together, inevitably end in sensuality and orgies.

It is true that the feast of St John, which comes just at the time when the Sun enters Cancer—a sign that is ruled by Venus—is not a celebration of spiritual fire. It celebrates physical, terrestrial fire. *Uriel* is the archangel of *Malkuth*, the earthly sphere, and the fire which he rules is not only that which ripens the harvests of fruit and grain, it is also the inner fire of the planet which maintains a great body of matter in a state of fusion in which minerals and metals are elaborated. This fire is often identified with the fires of hell.

In certain traditions summer is symbolized by a dragon with flames belching from its open jaws. This monster is the mythical animal that lives underground and appears on the surface only in order to burn, devour, and destroy. But it is also the guardian of all hidden treasure, symbolized by precious stones and metals, and the fruits of the earth; and those who wish to obtain these treasures must be capable of facing up to the dragon and defeating it. Here too, different traditions exist, many of which have come down to us in the form of fairy-tales and legends that tell of pure and daring heroes who conquer the dragon and take possession of its treasures. Disciples would do well to meditate on tales of this kind; the fact that the summer releases subterranean forces is no reason to let themselves be devoured by the dragon.

Unfortunately, because summer is the time when most people take their holidays, it is becoming more and more the season for the release of the instincts, particularly for inner sloth and sensuality. You might say that this is normal, since it is nature itself that incites us to this. Our lower nature, yes. And it is now that you must understand the importance of the five planes of the sephiroth. If you remain on the lowest plane of *Malkuth*, Earth, you will obviously be engulfed by your instincts. But if you work inwardly to rise to a higher level of this sephirah and make contact with the Beatified Souls, the *Ishim*, with the archangel *Uriel*, and with the Lord, *Adonai Melek,* not only will you defeat the dragon, but you will take possession of its treasures, that is, the new spiritual powers that you will have earned through your work to overcome the dark forces within you.

Autumn is ruled by *Mikhaël*, the archangel of the Sun in the sephirah *Tiphareth. Mikhaël* is the most renowned of all the angels. His name means 'Who is like God?' Tradition tells us that Lucifer was the most exalted of all the archangels; so exalted that he began to think himself the equal of God and planned to dethrone him. Seeing this, another archangel rose up, crying, 'Who is like God?', which in Hebrew is *Mi* (who), *ka* (like), and *El* (God). And the Lord, when he saw this, said: 'Henceforth you shall be called *Mikhaël*, and you will be the captain of the heavenly armies.'

In the Old Testament *Mikhaël* is the archangel of all victories over evil. In the New Testament, particularly in Revelation, it is said that he will be the one to overcome the dragon. There is an old tradition which says that when Moses was dying, the devil tried to get hold of his body, and it was the archangel *Mikhaël* who fought him and snatched it from him. Many paintings and icons depict *Mikhaël* with a pair of scales in which he weighs the actions of a human being after his death. On one side are his good deeds and on the other his evil deeds. And the scene is observed by the devil, lying in wait to drag the sinner down to his infernal kingdom, but who is left to gnash his teeth in fury as he sees *Mikhaël* adding one last good deed that tips the scales to the side of good.

The beginning of autumn coincides with the entrance of the Sun into the constellation of Libra. Autumn is the harvest season. The fruits of the earth are gathered, and those that are tainted are discarded and those that are good are kept. Jesus said: 'You will know a man by his fruits,' and there is a sense in which you can say that every harvest is a judgement. In nature, as in all of life, autumn is the best season, the season of fruits that have been ripened by the rays of the sun, of which *Mikhaël* is the archangel.

Finally, winter is under the aegis of *Gabriel*, the archangel of *Yesod*, which is the sephirah of the Moon. As winter begins we celebrate Christmas, the feast of the birth of Christ. The archangel *Gabriel* has a close link with the birth of children, the Moon, and the season of winter.

It was *Gabriel* who announced to Zacharias the birth of a son who would be called John the Baptist. It was also *Gabriel* who announced the birth of Jesus to Mary:

> *The angel Gabriel was sent by God to a town in Galilee called Nazareth, to a virgin engaged to a man whose name was Joseph, of the house of David. The virgin's name was Mary. And he came to her and said, 'Greetings, favoured one! The Lord is with you.' But she was much perplexed by his words and pondered what sort of greeting this might be. The angel said to her, 'Do not be afraid, Mary, for you have found favour with God. And now, you will conceive in your*

> *womb and bear a son, and you will name him Jesus.*

What is a birth? It is the passage from the invisible to the visible, from the immaterial to the material, from the abstract to the concrete. And it is the Moon, feminine principle *par excellence*, that presides over all forms of birth, whether on the physical or on the spiritual plane. During winter, when the nights are longer and the pulse of nature beats more slowly, conditions are less propitious to manifestations on the external plane, and more propitious to a more intense inner life. Human beings are stimulated to turn inwards and prepare the birth of that child of light, which, in some traditions, is symbolized by a pearl. Pearls come from the sea, and like the sea they have a special relationship with the Moon. On the Sephirotic Tree, the oyster that contains the pearl is *Yesod*, which represents the genital organs of the cosmic body. It is in this region that a pearl must be formed, for this pearl represents the very quintessence of love. The oyster is the feminine principle that brings to birth a pearl, that is, a child.

To summarize, the four seasons are presided over by four archangels: spring is under the influence of *Raphaël*, the archangel of *Hod*; summer is under the influence of *Uriel*, the archangel of *Malkuth*; autumn is influenced by *Mikhaël*, the archangel of *Tiphareth,* and winter is influenced by *Gabriel,* the archangel of *Yesod.* And now let us see where they fit on the Sephirotic Tree. Starting from below and working upwards, we have *Malkuth,* the Earth; *Yesod,* the Moon; *Hod,* Mercury, and *Tiphareth,* the Sun, in other words, the four elements: earth, water (the Moon), air (Mercury), and fire (the Sun). Now that you know these correspondences, you can learn to work with the four seasons, and in this way your life will become more and more rich in meaning.[2]

---

[2] In this connection, see chapter 17, *The Cardinal Feasts*, in vol. 32 of the Complete Works.

Chapter Thirteen

THE SEPHIROTIC TREE

SYMBOL OF SYNARCHIC ORDER

Throughout the course of history, human beings have always hoped to find the perfect form of government, and this hope has led to many different experiments with monarchies, republics, oligarchies, and so on. I have already talked to you about a form of government known as 'synarchy', popularized in the West by the writings of Saint-Yves d'Alveydre. According to this author, a synarchic government is composed of three individuals who together represent the supreme authority in the State. Under the direction of this authority, there is a group of seven who represent the executive. And under this group of seven, there are twelve persons in charge of the economy, that is, of the production and distribution of wealth.

In reality, as I have already pointed out, as long as a synarchy remains a purely external form of government, it cannot be the solution to every problem. The mere fact that there are three, then seven, then twelve at the head of a country or collectivity, will not automatically ensure that everything runs smoothly, for those three, seven, and twelve might well be ambitious, dishonest, or irrational people who would lead the country to ruin just as easily as any others. The solution is not in the numbers, but in the human beings themselves, in the qualities they possess. This is why I continue to insist that before making any attempt to establish a synarchy on the physical plane, each human being must work to establish it within themselves.

You will be wondering what this means. How is it possible to establish a synarchic government within oneself? Well, each one of you has a mind, a heart, and a will. Your mind enables you to think; with your heart you experience feelings and emotions; and your will urges you to act. These are the three elements through which you manifest yourself in the world. When you succeed in establishing wisdom in your mind, love in your heart, and strength in your will, you achieve within yourself a trinity that likens you to the divine Trinity of light, warmth, and life, and links you to *Kether*, *Chokmah*, and *Binah*. In this way you become your own supreme authority and reign over your own existence. And you govern by manifesting the virtues of the seven planets, that is, the seven sephiroth: *Chesed* (Jupiter), *Geburah* (Mars), *Tiphareth* (the Sun), *Netzach* (Venus), *Hod* (Mercury), *Yesod* (the Moon), and *Malkuth* (Earth). These are the seven qualities that represent the executive. Thus it is you who are the authority, and through your qualities and virtues you exercise your executive powers. It is our qualities and virtues that are our most faithful servants. Our true servants are not those we employ to satisfy our desires and needs or to make life easier; they are the inner virtues that are obedient to the true authority of *Kether*, *Chokmah*, and *Binah*. These virtues are the capacity for realization of *Malkuth*, the purity of *Yesod*, the intelligence of *Hod*, the tenderness of *Netzach*, the beauty of *Tiphareth*, the audacity of *Geburah*, and the generosity of *Chesed*. These are the seven servants who transmit orders from the supreme authority to the twelve who are in charge of the economic sphere.

What does the economic sphere correspond to? The economic sphere is represented by the twelve divisions of our physical body, which are linked to the twelve signs of the zodiac: the head (Aries), the neck (Taurus), the arms and lungs (Gemini), the stomach (Cancer), the heart (Leo), the solar plexus (Virgo), the kidneys (Libra), the sexual organs (Scorpio), the thighs

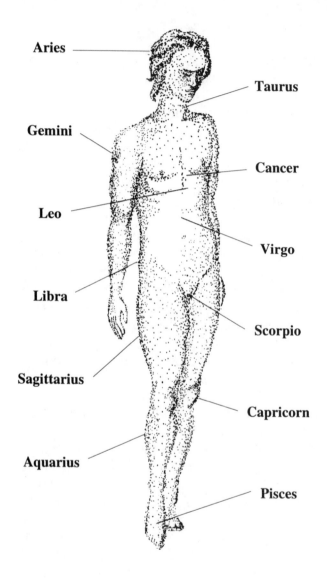

(Sagittarius), the knees (Capricorn), the calves (Aquarius), and the feet (Pisces). Thus the seven virtues act upon the different parts of the body, stimulating and vivifying them, and ensuring that the billions of cells of which they are constituted contribute to the harmony of the whole. This then is the true synarchy, the only kind that you should be concerned with: the synarchy within. As for synarchy as a form of government—do you think it is possible to find three people in every country who are sufficiently highly evolved to assume authority? And what about the seven executives, who must be truly capable of not only understanding the decisions of the first three, but of seeing that they are carried out correctly? Even if such persons were to be found, do you think that they would be accepted by the majority?

If we want to establish peace and harmony in the world we have to begin at the beginning, and the beginning is ourselves, human beings. True synarchy will be established only when each one of us is the head, the king of our own realm, of our own population, and, first and most important, of our own thoughts, feelings, and actions. Otherwise we are the servants, the slaves, of our vices and weaknesses.

Here again, as you see, the Sephirotic Tree offers us a working method, it shows us the path to follow; it helps us to understand what true synarchy is and how to achieve it.

Chapter Fourteen

YESOD

FOUNDATION OF THE SPIRITUAL LIFE

I

A great many people have come to me at different times, hoping that I would give them easy ways to develop psychic faculties, magical powers, and so on. When I told them that the most effective way of obtaining such powers was to purify oneself, to do a thorough spring-cleaning of one's inner self, they turned away immediately—and you should have seen the scorn on their faces! What I had said seemed to them altogether too puerile. They went off to ask someone else to help them, convinced that they would eventually find what they were looking for. Of course, they will certainly find something, and what that will be hardly bears thinking about! But you must try to understand that purity is the most effective way to achieve realizations on the spiritual plane, for once the ground is cleared and the way opened to the celestial currents, there will be nothing to prevent them from reaching you and giving you what you ask for.

Unfortunately, most people who turn to spirituality imagine that an initiatic teaching will give them the satisfaction and success they have failed to find by other means. No, an initiatic teaching will never give them this, and if they try to make use of the occult sciences to achieve their personal aims, they will have to pay very dearly for it. If I could be sure that I had been able to make you understand only this, I would consider that I had achieved a large part of my task.

I gave a series of talks one year on the subject of purity, taking as my starting point the sephirah *Yesod*, in order to show you how vast and profound this question is, and how it touches on areas that people rarely think about.[1] Everyone knows the difficulties that can be caused by blocked pipes and dirty windows or spectacles, but very few ever think that they are harbouring those same problems within themselves: thoughts, feelings, and desires which are like stains, dust, or rubbish clogging their spiritual channels and preventing divine light from reaching and entering them. You can build nothing solid and durable in the

---

[1]   See *The Mysteries of Yesod*, Complete Works, vol. 7.

spiritual life unless you begin by working to purify yourself.

But you must not think that I insist so much on purity because it is the only thing you need to think about, or because you need never seek any further than this. No, not at all! If I insist on purity it is because it is the foundation of all the rest—this is what *Yesod* means, base or foundation. And the function of a foundation is to bear the weight of the whole edifice. All the other sephiroth on the Tree of Life represent virtues with which disciples must also learn to work, but the work with *Yesod*, the foundation, represents the condition that must be fulfilled before you can begin to learn or to create in the spiritual world.

Why is *Yesod* represented as the basis of all spiritual life? Because the psychic world begins with *Yesod*. We saw this when we studied the four divisions of the Sephirotic Tree:

> *Atziluth*, comprised of *Kether, Chokmah,* and *Binah*, which corresponds to the divine world.
> *Briah*, comprised of *Chesed, Geburah,* and *Tiphareth*, which corresponds to the spiritual world.
> *Yetzirah,* comprising *Netzach, Hod,* and *Yesod*, which corresponds to the psychic world.

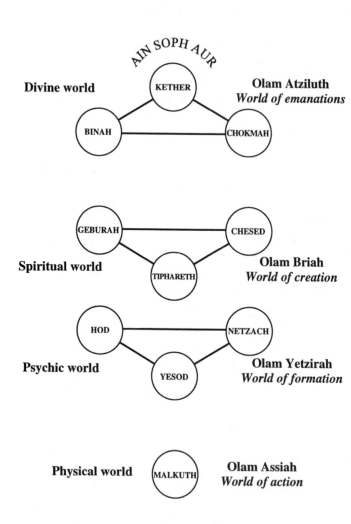

The Sephirotic Tree

Assiah, formed by *Malkuth* alone, which corresponds to the physical world.

As soon as one leaves *Malkuth*, the physical world, one crosses the threshold into the psychic world, of which *Yesod* is the first degree. Like all the other sephiroth, *Yesod* has its own inner hierarchy, and the lower levels correspond to the Moon, which, in psychology, represents the world of the unconscious, of instincts, imagination, and illusions. Thus it is essential to make oneself master of this world, so as to bring order and light into it. And this is what it means to purify oneself. It is as simple as that. Yes, to purify oneself is, first of all, to be capable of recognizing the nature of what goes on in one's own inner life, of analysing one's thoughts, feelings, desires, and ambitions, and of working to make them less selfish and more generous.

In spite of these explanations, I know that many will close their ears, justifying their rejection of what I say with the argument that purity means bigotry, restriction, fanaticism, and even exclusion; that in the name of purity people have been persecuted, massacred and burned at the stake. Really? But have not such terrible crimes also been committed in the name of love? Does that prevent them from pronouncing the word or from continuing to love? What a hypocritical argument! They are ready to take anything as an excuse not to exert themselves. On the pretext that the notion of purity has so often been misunderstood they continue to churn up all kinds of dirt. Well, they are free to do so, of course, but one day they will see the results of their distorted way of thinking.

Those who have never learned to work with *Yesod* will never get beyond the psychic world; they will never know the reality of the spiritual world. Even if—as is sometimes the case—they have genuine psychic gifts, they must realize that that is not enough. They must understand that the psychic world is not the spiritual world, and that although they have a psychic talent, they do not necessarily know how to make good use of it. Musicians and painters, however highly talented, will never make anything of their gifts if they do not subject themselves to discipline and study under the guidance of a master. An artistic gift has to be cultivated; so does a psychic gift. Those who possess such gifts need to work towards purity, the one quality that can give them true discernment and enable them to exert a beneficial influence. And in this context purity means not only clear-sightedness, but also honesty, selflessness, and a sense of responsibility.

But what do we usually see in these cases? Suppose someone has a precognitive dream, in which he senses that he or someone else is in danger, or that such and such an event is going to take place. He is so pleased to discover that he has a gift that is a subject of wonder to all his friends that he proclaims himself a clairvoyant, opens his own office, and gives consultations to countless people who are worried about themselves or their families. And little by little, this new clairvoyant begins to deliver 'messages from heaven'. Does it ever occur to him to wonder whether he is really fit to make such claims? Oh no, as long as he has had a few precognitive dreams or a few intuitions that turned out to be accurate, he imagines that he is capable of answering people's questions, whatever they may be and whenever they ask them, and that he is never wrong. Unfortunately, he is deluding himself. Those who seriously want to develop the gift of clairvoyance must work with great vigilance every day to keep their psychic world in order; otherwise they will end by being in such a state of inner confusion that they will deceive both themselves and others. Many, many people have embarked on the path of mediumship without preparation or precautions of any kind and have ended by going out of their minds.[2]

---

[2] See *Looking into the Invisible*, Izvor Collection No. 228.

This is why sensible, rational people, particularly scientists, refuse to entertain any discussion of psychic powers and faculties— they immediately think of all these charlatans and cranks. Of course, they are right not to take just anyone's word for it, but they are not right to allow themselves to be put off by such manifestations and refuse to look into the question any further, or to study and try to understand the psychic realm. In doing this they are limiting their reflection and investigations, and, on the pretext of common sense and objectivity, they look no further than external appearances. Of course, I know that there are some serious scientists who are interested in what they call 'parapsychological phenomena', but most of them would not admit to it for fear of being discredited by their colleagues. This is also true of many priests and clergymen who believe in reincarnation but never say so, because reincarnation is not accepted by the Church and they do not want to attract censure. It is regrettable that more scientists and clergy do not have a greater sense of responsibility, for they are allowing many people, who are searching and in danger of losing their way, to continue to grope in the dark.

Nothing is going to stop people today from wanting to find something other than what conventional science or the approved doctrine of the Church gives them. But they are in great danger of getting bogged down in the lower regions of *Yesod*. This is why it is so important for them really to understand what purity is, for it is the key to the spiritual life.

When you work seriously and in depth to purify yourself, light can flow into you more and more easily, and you begin to see more clearly, to be more lucid. The sickly, ailing particles in your body are eliminated and your physical health begins to improve; the weak particles hampering your will are also discarded and you become stronger. All that is dark and shadowy begins to disappear. If you were sad, you find yourself filled with joy, for joy is simply an aspect of purity; and the more you purify yourself, the more you will feel light-hearted, gay, and joyful. And just as impurity leads to putrefaction, fermentation, dislocation, and death, the exact opposite happens when you purify yourself: you draw closer to immortality. Thus health, power, knowledge, happiness, and immortality are simply different aspects of purity.

This summarizes the whole of initiatic science; it is up to you now to verify it for yourselves.

II

On the central pillar of the Sephirotic Tree, *Yesod* is above *Malkuth*, and *Tiphareth* is above *Yesod*. From this we can deduce that the light of *Tiphareth* (the Sun) has to pass through *Yesod* (the Moon) in order to reach *Malkuth* (Earth). We are speaking here of *Malkuth* as the symbolic representation of the physical world, of *Yesod* as representing the psychic world, and of *Tiphareth* as representing the spiritual world. And now we can see the problems that must arise if the state of the psychic world is not sufficiently pure to allow the light of the spiritual world to pass through it.

Unfortunately, this is the case with most people. They complain of feeling no benefits from their spiritual exercises. They pray, they meditate, they try to link themselves to heaven, but they have the impression that none of it does them any good. They feel just as doubtful, disorientated, and weak as ever. Sometimes they even feel that their situation is worse than before. All of this is because the light to which they are trying to link themselves encounters too many layers of impurity, formed by their untidy, undisciplined thoughts and feelings. In this case, not only is it prevented from entering them, but it actually accelerates the process of putrefaction that is going on within them, just as sunlight accelerates the putrefaction of a heap of compost.

Rays of sunlight can reach and illuminate us if our windows are clean, but when they have to penetrate layers of impurities, they trigger a process of putrefaction. And putrefaction produces nauseating smells. If you want to become a worthy receptacle for divine light, your heart must be as transparent as crystal; if it is not, the smell of putrefaction is what awaits you. As long as you have not made up your mind to do any serious work of detachment and purification, you would do better not to approach initiatic science. I warn you of this because it would be useless, later on, to blame that science for your problems; they will be your own fault, entirely your own fault.

Once you have really begun to work with *Yesod*, the light of *Tiphareth* will circulate within you, and it is this light that will enable you to understand the reality of things and to orientate yourself correctly. When this light is not within you, you are obliged to rely on others for support and advice on every aspect of your life. And as there is no guarantee that their ideas or judgement will really enlighten you, you will be at the mercy of contradictory opinions.

To be truly wealthy is to possess this light that enables you to discover the truth for yourself without always being obliged to consult others. 'Without even being obliged to consult a spiritual master or an initiate?' you will ask. Yes, why not? If you are capable of being equal or even superior to them, why not? Of course, it will be a long and difficult process, but there is no decree of cosmic intelligence that says you will always have to be limited and dependent. Disciples have never been forbidden to equal or even surpass their master. The path is always open to you; indeed it may well be the only one that is truly open. Nobody can prevent you from growing and advancing in light. Why else would Jesus have said: 'Be perfect, therefore, as your heavenly Father is perfect?'

When travelling through the territory of *Yesod*, disciples need a guide more than at any other time. But once they have gone beyond *Yesod*, the way is open and they can go on alone, for they have reached the region of light that bestows true clairvoyance.

Do not be deceived, the only true clairvoyance is that which enables you to see the reality of the spiritual world, in other words, to perceive and understand all that is most subtle in nature and in the human soul. The other kind of clairvoyance consists in seeing past or future events, or the spirits of the astral world, and there is nothing very remarkable about it. Everybody, or almost everybody, can obtain this kind of clairvoyance by means of drugs or certain exercises, but such means will not get anyone very far; moreover they are very dangerous for one's psychic balance. The only kind of clairvoyance you should seek is that which will transform you into a prism of crystal through which the light of heaven can pass. It was this clairvoyance that Jesus was speaking of when he said: 'Blessed are the pure of heart, for they shall see God.'

In the sephirah *Yesod*, God is named *El Hai*, which means Living God. In *Yesod* God manifests himself as the creator and giver of life, but of life at its purest: the life that flows from on high, from the source, cleansing and purifying all in its path. For the first task accomplished by life is precisely this: the elimination of all the impure elements that prevent it from flowing freely.

And as God is present in every sephirah, to see God also means to receive the blessings contained in each of the sephiroth: the science of *Hod*, the grace of *Netzach*, the splendour of *Tiphareth*, the strength of *Geburah*, the generosity of *Chesed*, the stability of *Binah*, the wisdom of *Chokmah*, and finally the omnipotence of *Kether*. Each sephirah corresponds to a divine virtue, and you can work with any of them, but you must always remember that you will get no benefit from doing so if you do not begin by working with *Yesod*. In any case, those who try to obtain the virtues or powers of the other sephiroth without first working with *Yesod* will be prevented from advancing. They will be left to stagnate in the swamps of the astral plane, where they will experience only illusions, disappointment, and torment.

Make up your minds not to base your life on the acquisition of knowledge, wealth, or power, but on purity, and one day you will possess more than knowledge, more than wealth, more than power. History records many examples of men and women, who, never having studied or read a book, worked exclusively at achieving purity, and ended by manifesting all the other qualities as well:

wisdom, clairvoyance, the power of healing, and so on. They had rid themselves of all their inner layers of opacity, all their inner obstacles, and the treasures of heaven were able to pour into them.

Yesod is the beginning of the psychic life, and in this sense it would be true to say that magic begins with the sephirah *Yesod*. True magic resides in our thoughts and feelings. Wands, pantacles, and talismans are not necessary; all magical power lies in the potency of our psychic life. This is why the Moon, which belongs to the sphere of *Yesod*, is the 'star' of magic. Those who want to possess the true powers of magic must begin by purifying their psychic world. They must understand that the greatest of all magical powers is purity, for it is through *Yesod* that we gain access to the mysteries.

Chapter Fifteen

BINAH

I

THE LAWS OF DESTINY

Binah is the first sephirah on the left-hand pillar of the Sephirotic Tree. This pillar is known as *Boaz*, the Pillar of Severity, and it represents the feminine principle in creation. In this sephirah God manifests himself as *Jehovah*, the terrible God that revealed himself to Moses. The whole of the Old Testament resounds with his wrath, with the threats and maledictions with which he cursed human beings 'even unto the fourth generation'. It was to this all-consuming fire that the Hebrews offered countless animals in sacrifice in the hope of appeasing his wrath. Moses, too, like all the patriarchs and prophets, raised his voice in supplication, imploring the Lord to turn away the chastisement with which he threatened his people.

You will be wondering how this terrible God can be a feminine power. The answer is that this feminine power is nature. You will certainly understand this better if you think about what nature really is, if you remember that she is a stern and implacable mother. Nature has created certain laws, and if you break those laws you are bound to be punished in one way or another. And that punishment may also strike your children and grand-children. All this is very easy to understand. Take one of the most obvious examples, that of alcoholism. If you want to remain both physically and psychologically healthy you must drink no more than a limited amount of alcohol. You all know what happens to someone who exceeds the limit—no need for me to enlarge on this—and this person will pass on to his children a tainted heredity. The same can be said of all excesses, all transgressions of the natural law.

In spite of the impressive progress that has been made in medical science and technology and the innumerable medicines that are now available, if human beings do not behave sensibly, if they fail to respect certain laws, they will continue to suffer—and make others suffer—in one way or another. Even so, many people are indignant at what they consider to be the cruelty of a God who punishes not only the sinner but also the sinner's descendants as well. But this God is nature, for nature is not something that exists outside or apart from

God. God is a severe mother who lays down certain limits beyond which her children must not go. If they go beyond these limits we say that she punishes them, but actually it is they who, in breaking out of the protective enclosure in which they were sheltered, have put themselves and all those who depend on them in jeopardy.

You will perhaps object that this portrayal of a mother is not one that you are used to. On the contrary, you like to picture a mother as someone who is always loving and indulgent; it is the father who is severe. But this shows that you have not been sufficiently observant, and have not really thought it through. What is the role of a mother in respect to a small child? She has to feed it, of course, but as soon as possible she also has to teach it what it must do or not do in order to grow and develop as it should. She teaches it to observe the rules of nutrition and hygiene, and warns it of certain dangers. She refuses it certain things, holds it back from the dangers of fire or water, takes matches or sharp things away from it, hides the sweets and jam it is over-fond of, and so on. Sometimes she keeps an eye on it from a distance while allowing it to go its own way, and then if it falls and hurts itself, she says: 'You see what happens when you do that! Don't do it; otherwise you will only hurt yourself again.'

And when her child is really capricious and goes too far she punishes it.

The role of a mother in respect to a small child can be compared with the role of nature in respect to all human beings. Some of you will say that they have seen fathers who have assumed this role, because the mothers... Yes, I have seen that too, but here we are talking about principles, not particular cases. On the level of principles it is the mother who has nature's role as the educator of her child. And this is how you must envisage the role of the cosmic Mother, who manifests herself in *Binah* under the aspect of *Jehovah*.

The sephirah *Binah* reveals to us the mysteries of destiny, because it enlightens us about the law of cause and effect. Many people think that life is absurd and that there is nothing logical about events or people's destinies; but that is because they do not possess the elements that would enable them to see and understand. These elements are to be found in *Binah*, for the angelic hierarchy at work here is the *Aralim*, or Thrones, those that St John saw in his vision in the form of twenty-four Elders. The Twenty-four Elders are also known as the Lords of Destiny, because it is they who examine the way each individual has lived in previous incarnations and determine his destiny according to his merits. Their decrees are carried out either by the angels of *Chesed*, the *Hashmalim*—who dispense rewards—or the angels of *Geburah*, the *Seraphim*—who administer punishment.

What is destiny? Destiny is an archetypal form, and each individual lives his life according to the form that destiny assigns to him. The Twenty-four Elders represent the divine tribunal that decrees the forms of human destinies, and the physical forms that we see on earth are simply a faint reflection of the those that have been decreed on high. One of these forms is projected into the womb of every pregnant woman, and it is this form that provides the basis for the work of gestation. Once these forms are decreed there is no changing them; they descend to the material plane on which they take on physical form.

Destiny can be changed, therefore, only by changing the archetypes. There is no other way. It is useless to consult astrologers in the hope of learning in advance about future trials and difficulties so that you can take precautionary measures to avoid them. Everything is ordained in such a way that what must be will be. In order to change one's destiny one has to reach the regions beyond *Binah*, in other words, the regions that are above and beyond destiny, the regions of *Chokmah* and *Kether*. This is possible. There have been human beings of such exceptional virtue that they were freed from the laws of destiny. But imagine the work they must have done to reach such a level! As far as we are concerned, the only way to ensure the forbearance of the Lords of Destiny is to accept their decrees with love and humility, in the knowledge that they are perfectly just, because they are the consequence of our past incarnations. The wisest course is to consider the difficulties and trials of this life as so many problems that we have been given to resolve, and to remember that they offer us the most effective means of evolution.

The inflexible character of *Binah* is seen also in the symbolism of Saturn, which is portrayed as an old man—sometimes as a skeleton—carrying a scythe. The scythe of Saturn represents time, which destroys everything; and the skeleton represents eternity, that which resists the attack of time. Thus Saturn represents both aspects. Beyond the domain of the flesh, the world of external appearances that is continually being destroyed by time (the scythe), is the indestructible skeleton (eternity). But many, many hours and years of reflection and meditation are necessary before we can understand how to make the passage from time to eternity.

Saturn says little and listens a great deal, because the ability to hear and listen is necessary for understanding. Those who know how to listen are on the way to understanding. In this sense one could say that to 'hear' is to understand what we listen to.[1] The quality of Saturn is the capacity to listen, and not only to listen to the counsels of the wise or the sounds of nature, but to hear something more, to discern the voice within. It is when we listen in this way that the subtlest realities, those that rise from the depths of our being, make themselves heard. It is then that the voice of intuition, the voice of God—the voice of silence, as it is sometimes called—reaches us. This is why true Saturnians love to get away from noise and withdraw to a solitary place to listen to the voice of silence, the voice that enables them to free themselves from the laws of time and enter the realm of eternity.

---

[1] Omraam Mikhaël Aïvanhov uses the French verb '*entendre*', which means both to hear and to understand. In other words, it is not enough to hear, in the ordinary sense of the word, nor even to listen: we have to 'hear' the inner meaning of what we listen to. (Translator's note)

II

THE REALM OF STABILITY

Even those who have embraced the spiritual life find it difficult to rise to a higher level of consciousness, and above all to remain at that level. They may succeed one day, but the day after they relax their attention. It is almost impossible to achieve a state that is truly stable, that never changes. Stability is the apogee of initiation, the point at which a disciple can echo the words of the hierophants of ancient Egypt: 'I am stable, the son of he who is stable, conceived and engendered in the realm of stability.' The realm of stability is *Binah*, the realm of the Twenty-four Elders.

What exactly is stability? It is the quality of one who can no longer be daunted or overcome by evil. And to avoid being overcome by evil one has to escape its clutches by rising to a region where it no longer has any power. You will ask: 'But do such regions truly exist?' Yes, they exist: they exist within you, and they exist in the universe. If you have not already realized this it is because you are not in the habit of observing yourself. Have you never been surprised to notice that if some incident that once had the power to sadden and discourage you occurs in different circumstances it no longer distresses you in the same way? Why is this? Is it because you have lost all feeling? No, it is because you have managed to rise to a level of consciousness that puts you out of reach of that distress. This is sure proof that there are regions within a human being in which they cannot be reached by evil.

The Cabbalah says that the serpent can rise only to certain sephiroth, but that it can never reach the region formed by *Kether*, *Chokmah*, and *Binah*. And since we are created in the image of the universe, there is a region within us, too, in which evil cannot exist. The conditions it needs are not there. Within the sublime regions of our being and of the universe there is such light and such intensity of vibrations that anything that is not in harmony with that purity and light simply disintegrates. Evil is not allowed to exist in these sublime regions; it is rejected; it can exist only in the lower regions. For it is only in the lower regions of matter that it finds the conditions it needs to move freely, cause havoc, and make people unhappy. Depending on which region you find yourself in, therefore, you will be either vulnerable or immune to the onslaught of evil. This is what initiatic science teaches us. And this is what Jesus meant when he said that a wise man builds his house on a rock. Symbolically, the rock is that inner region that Hindu philosophy calls the causal plane, and which is beyond the astral and mental planes, beyond the plane of our ordinary thoughts and feelings.

The Twenty-four Elders mentioned by St John in the Apocalypse are seated on unshakeable rocks ('Around the throne are twenty-four thrones, and seated on the thrones are Twenty-four Elders, dressed in white robes...'). Stability is the essence of God himself. God is in essence unchangeable: unchangeable in his love, in his wisdom, and in his power.

If you want to approach the stability of the Twenty-four Elders, you must never abandon your high ideal. Once you have decided to tread the path of light, you must always, whatever the circumstances, continue in the same direction. You can change everything else, but you must never abandon your divine orientation. You must be sure to understand that stability does not signify immobility. If you meet a true spiritual master, you will see that he never remains motionless, like an idol, waiting for his disciples to kiss his hands or feet. On the contrary, he is always active, always on the go—more than most people, in fact—moving about in order to visit those who need him, and to instruct and heal them. His stability is within, in his convictions; nobody can seduce him with wealth or honours.

To be stable is to be true to one's commitments and to persevere on one's chosen path in spite of all obstacles. And this is difficult, much more difficult than to be nice and kind, helpful, cheerful, generous, and courageous. When you are feeling generous you give your word and make promises, but a few days later you find yourself in a different frame of mind and do not even remember the promises you made. Well, this is not the way to gain access to the real powers of the region of *Binah*.

The truth is that human beings are none too eager to hear talk of fidelity and stability. Oh how boring! Oh how difficult! Well, let me tell you that if you have this attitude, these virtues will seem even more boring and even more difficult to realize. It is you who determine what qualities you will have. What does that mean? It means that when you do not like a particular quality you will not attract it. You do not like fidelity, you prefer variety—so how can you expect stability to come and dwell in you? When I analyse this question I find that it is human beings themselves who repulse this or that virtue, simply because they do not like it. If you want to attract something to yourself you have to love it. This is the magical side of things. Before attempting to obtain something—anything at all—try to begin by loving it, otherwise all your efforts will be in vain. It is absolutely essential to know this law.

Try to develop a love of stability. Try to become more faithful to your ideal. Try never to betray it under any pretext, otherwise the great spirits who observe your actions will lose confidence in you. And if they no longer appreciate or respect you, they will stop helping you. If this happens, if you are left to your own resources, you will not be able to accomplish much. However fond of change you may be— and there is absolutely no reason why you should not change your activities—you must never abandon your high ideal. You can be in favour of external diversity, but you must be sure to maintain inner unity.[1]

---

[1]   See 'From Multiplicity to Unity', in *In Spirit and in Truth*, Izvor Collection No. 235.

Chapter Sixteen

CHOKMAH

THE CREATIVE WORD

'In the beginning was the Word...' The opening words of the Gospel of St John have given rise to innumerable commentaries. It is, of course, totally impossible to understand exactly what it means to say that God created the world by his Word. But as that which is below is like that which is above... as we are created in the image of God and of the universe, it is possible, by studying the power of our own words, whether written or spoken, to have some faint notion of the power of the divine Word.

When a general gives the order to attack, he cries 'Fire!' and within minutes a magnificent city is reduced to rubble. The general himself did nothing concrete, he simply said one word, but what power in that word! Or suppose a man or woman means a great deal to you, but you

have no idea whether they reciprocate your
feelings, and then you suddenly get a letter
from them that says, 'I love you.' Nothing has
changed and yet everything has changed: your
life is suddenly illuminated!

Everything that exists points to the power
of words. What do you think usually motivates
people to talk? It is the desire to exercise
power. Even when they seem to be explaining
something or giving information, they are not
really motivated by the desire to explain or
inform. They are seeking to produce some
specific effect—to arouse their audience to
anger or hatred, for instance, or to allay
suspicion. What about yourselves? Do you
never do the same? Yes, you do—I leave you to
think about this.

Let us return to the opening words of St
John's Gospel: 'In the beginning was the
Word.' Human beings would save themselves a
great deal of difficulty and suffering if they
knew how to apply this phrase to their lives.
You will say: 'But it is so abstract and difficult
to understand. How can it be applied?' Ah, but
it is precisely because you never try to apply it
that it remains abstract and difficult to
understand. 'So what should we do? How can
we apply it?' You can apply it by
accompanying all your actions with the Word.

Take a very simple example from everyday life. When you wash your windows, instead of letting your thoughts wander in all directions, be conscious of your gestures and accompany them with words. You can say, for instance: 'As I wash this window, may my heart be washed and become perfectly transparent!' And when you are sweeping the floor, dusting, or doing the washing up, you can say something similar. And if you drop and break something, say: 'May every obstacle on my way to God break into a thousand pieces!'

Of course, you do not have to say any of this aloud, especially if there is a chance of someone else hearing you! The important thing is to be conscious, that is, to apply your thought—and thought necessarily implies words—to all your actions so as to become truly creative. For those who live a spiritual life, this is the significance of these words: 'In the beginning was the Word... All things came into being through him, and without him not one thing came into being.' You must always place the Word at the beginning so as to ensure that all your activity moves in the right direction. But this is a notion that even believers have not yet understood. They recite their prayers several times a day, but they are ready-made prayers, which they have learned by heart and which they mutter to themselves while thinking of something else. It is not necessary to recite a lot of prayers by heart. For Christians, the Lord's Prayer and two or three others are enough. Beyond that it is up to each individual to say a few words within themselves depending on circumstances and the changing events in their lives. There is no better way of understanding what the omnipotence of the divine Word means.

When the wind blows away the clouds and the impurities in the atmosphere, ask that the breath of the spirit may blow away all your bad thoughts and feelings. When you see the sun coming up over the horizon, say: 'As the sun rises over the world, may the sun of love rise in my heart, may the sun of wisdom rise in my intelligence, may the sun of truth rise in my soul and spirit.' This is how you will become a true child of God: through the divine Word. For the Word is alive and active and has the power to transform you.

Once you begin to understand the meaning of the words, 'In the beginning was the Word,' you will also understand why it is said that: 'In the beginning God created heaven and earth,' and what lies behind these two words, heaven and earth, and the relationship between the two, and how we should work with them. Heaven and earth are within us, and as long as we separate them, as long as we fail to join heaven—our thought—to earth—our everyday activities—we shall never know what the living Word of God is.[1]

---

[1] See chapter 11 of *The Fruits of the Tree of Life*, vol. 32 of the Complete Works.

Chapter Seventeen

YESOD, TIPHARETH, KETHER

THE SUBLIMATION OF SEXUAL ENERGY

The name of God in the sephirah *Yesod* is *Shadai El Hai*, and *El Hai*, as we have seen, means Living God. *Yesod* is the only sephirah in which life is mentioned as an attribute of the Deity. It is implied, of course, in the others, but in *Yesod* it is made explicit. And since it is God who bears the name 'living', it means that the life that manifests itself in *Yesod* is of the utmost purity. *Yesod*, the foundation, is the sephirah of pure life, and in the figure of cosmic man, Adam Kadmon, it represents the genital organs, because it is these organs that create life.

Although we are bound to admit that human beings are not particularly concerned with purity in relation to their sexual life, the truth remains that cosmic intelligence has decreed that the purity of *Yesod* shall manifest itself through the sexual organs.

Nowadays people say that sexual morals have been 'liberated', as though this represented great progress. This liberation could have meant real progress, but the reality of what we see today is not a step forward: it is a regression. The growing tendency of people to sleep together simply because they know no better way of passing the time and having pleasure is very detrimental to their evolution. They do not know each other, they have barely met each other, they do not love each other, and they 'make love', just for want of anything better to do, as though it were of no more importance than playing cards! And when they have finished—just as when they have finished playing cards—they go their separate ways and begin again the next day with someone else. What they are doing is seriously wrong. And it is wrong not because they are flouting certain rules of behaviour invented by the moralizers, but because they are injuring themselves. There is nothing reprehensible in the act of sexual intercourse itself, even if it is not for the purpose of procreation, but it is essential to know about all the entities and forces involved in this act, in order to give it a divine meaning and orientation.

Those who practise sexual intercourse simply for the sake of the pleasure it gives them are not only squandering their energies, but they are also allowing entities of the lower astral plane to feed on them. As long as a man and woman are in a room with the door shut while they are making love, they think that they are alone. Not at all! They are accompanied by all kinds of invisible entities who come to feed on their emanations. If they are simply giving in to their sensuality, their emanations will feed larvae and elementals. But if they have prepared themselves in advance and are conscious of the sacredness of the sexual act, they will be accompanied by spirits of light who come not only to find nourishment, but also to give them many blessings. Knowing this, the disciples of an initiatic teaching take the initiative and invite heavenly entities to accompany them and to enlighten them, so that they may be capable of sublimating this act.

The entities who possess the secret of the sublimation of sexual energy are the *Malakhim,* the angels of *Tiphareth*, the Sun. The sexual energy of human beings is of the same nature as solar energy, but as they do not know this, they waste it and defile themselves by using it for the satisfaction of their passions. Once men and women are truly aware that this energy is impregnated with the light of the sun, they will set foot on the path of sanctity and begin to approach the sephirah *Kether*, in which the *Seraphim* sing without ceasing: 'Holy, holy,

holy, the Lord God the Almighty.' Only then will they begin to taste true love, the love of the *Seraphim*.

The sublimation of sexual energy follows a path that goes from *Yesod* to *Kether* by way of *Tiphareth*. The sanctity of *Kether*, the crowned head at the summit of the central pillar, takes its source in *Yesod*, the sexual organs. The sanctity of *Kether* is the sexual energy that a disciple endeavours to sublimate, thanks to the powers of *Tiphareth*, until it reaches the highest level and manifests itself as a golden radiance above his head. It is the goal of initiation to become capable of mastering the brute force that tries to drag us down, to turn it around and make it go in the opposite direction, and to work on that quintessence until it is transformed into an aura of light. Thus a true initiate is one who, thanks to the powers of *Tiphareth*, has realized within himself the purity of *Yesod*. An initiate has the same organs as all other human beings, and these organs produce the same matter, but this sublime matter takes the upward path to nourish his higher spiritual centres and to radiate over his head in the form of rays of light.

These are the truths that were taught to disciples of all the ancient initiations. In those days anybody who wished to have access to the mysteries was required to undergo years of study and hard work. And even then many were refused. All I ask of you is that you make an effort at least to be conscious of the value of the knowledge you receive, and to thank heaven for it.

Chapter Eighteen

THE PRAYER OF SOLOMON

PROSVETA

The Doves Nest
Duddleswell
Uckfield
TN22 3JJ

Omraam Mikhaël Aïvanhov

❏ I wish to be on your mailing list to receive free information on Prosveta's publications

❏ Please send me details of meetings and activities of the Universal White Brotherhood.

❏ I wish to support the work of Prosveta and enclose a donation herewith.
Book Distributors for the Universal White Brotherhood.   Registered Charity No. 288339

Name (Please print) ....

Address ....

Town ....   County ....

Postcode ....   Country ....

Some of you have asked me to recite the Prayer of Solomon, for they have never heard it. I can do this, of course. I have already done it a few times in the past, in exceptional circumstances, but before doing so today, I must say a few words of warning.

Nowadays, with esotericism and the occult sciences being all the fashion, more and more of the knowledge that has been kept secret for centuries is being made available to everybody. In the past these things were revealed only to those who had shown themselves worthy to receive them, but today they are exposed for all to see. And not only are they exposed, but they are all mixed up. True and false, good and bad, white magic and black: all this is made available to the general public, but the public is never taught how to distinguish the good from the bad, or warned about the terrible dangers that threaten those who launch themselves blindly into some of these disciplines and practices. So be very careful!

This prayer, said to be the Prayer of Solomon, is very potent because of all the divine names it invokes. One must not recite it without taking some precautions. Nobody is fit to address the sephiroth, the angelic hierarchies, and God himself, or to pronounce their names aloud if they have not already done a great deal of work on themselves. Indeed, even to hear these names, which are the most sacred in the Cabbalah, it is essential to have an inner attitude of great respect and reverence. This is the attitude I ask of you now.

Here is the prayer:

Powers of the Kingdom, be under my left foot and in my right hand.

Glory and Eternity, touch my two shoulders and guide me in the ways of Victory.

Mercy and Justice, be the balance and splendour of my life.

Understanding and Wisdom, give me the Crown.

Spirits of Malkuth, lead me between the two columns on which rests the edifice of the Temple.

Angels of Netzach and Hod, make me fast on the cubic stone of Yesod.

O Gedulaël! O Geburaël! O Tiphareth!

Binaël, be my love.

Ruah Chokmaël, be my light.

Be what you are and what you will be, O Ketheriel.

Ishim, help me in the name of Shaddai.

Kerubim, be my strength in the name of Adonai.

Bnei Elohim, be my brothers in the name of the Son and by the virtues of Tiphareth.

Elohim, fight for me in the name of the Tetragrammaton.

Malakhim, protect me in the name of Yahveh.

Seraphim, purify my love in the name of Eloha.

Hashmalim, enlighten me by the splendour of Elohim and the Shekinah.

Aralim, act.

Ophanim, turn and shine.

Hayoth HaKadesh, cry out, speak, roar, bellow.

Kadosh, Kadosh, Kadosh, Shaddai, Adonai.

Yod Heh Vau Heh.

Ehieh Asher Ehieh.

Alleluia, Alleluia, Alleluia.

Amen.

Now, the least you can do is prepare the best possible conditions of peace and purity within yourselves, so that you may give a fitting welcome to these exalted entities and so that they may respond to your appeal and bring you their help and their light. It is not enough to pronounce their names and call on them, even if you know the most propitious moment to do so. If you want them to pour down their blessings upon you, you must consecrate yourself and dedicate yourself to the service of the Godhead.

But how many people are capable of abandoning their prosaic concerns in order to scale these heights? Very few! This is why, even though these regions are the only ones in which I feel happy, I often give up the idea of talking to you about them. Very often, as I am on my way to the lecture hall, I think to myself:

'Today I'll talk to them about the Tree of Life and the angelic hierarchies.' Then I pronounce these names within myself. But when I get here and see your faces, I sense that there are so many other things you need to be told, so many things that are more urgent. How can I talk to you about such sublime realities when I can see in your eyes how deeply engrossed you still are in the cares of everyday life?

But today I have pronounced these divine names. They have flown away into space. The glorious hierarchies have heard me invoking them, and I ask them to give you all their blessings.[1]

---

[1] See chapter 1 of *The True Meaning of Christ's Teaching*, Izvor Collection No. 215, in which the Lord's Prayer is discussed in relation to the ten sephiroth.

Books by Omraam Mikhaël Aïvanhov
(Translated from the French)

Izvor Collection

Books by Omraam Mikhaël Aïvanhov
(Translated from the French)

Complete Works

Brochures:
New Presentation

Daily Meditations:
A thought for each day of the year.

Audio-cassettes:

Editor - Distributor

Editions PROSVETA S.A. — B.P. 12 — 83601 Fréjus Cedex (France)

Tel. 04 94 40 82 41 – Fax 04 94 40 80 05 – E-mail: international@prosveta.com

AGMV MARQUIS
Québec, Canada
1997